Testimonials

In *Altar Against Altar*, Andrew Mioni offered one of the clearest examinations of the traditionalist movement and its claims. With *Ignorance of Things Divine*, he follows up by contextualizing the crisis of faith among traditionalists, reaching back through centuries of papal teaching. Few writers combine such clarity of argument with historical depth. Mioni has proven himself to be one of the essential voices for understanding both the challenges we face and the remedy the Church herself proposes.

— Andrew Likoudis
Editor, *Faith in Crisis: Critical Dialogues in Catholic Traditionalism, Church Authority, and Reform*
Founder, Likoudis Legacy Foundation

This book does a thorough job outlining the current situation of the Church and the crisis that she faces. The research presented in this book strongly supports the thesis that the crisis is not the result of Vatican II but is rooted in challenges that cropped up in the centuries prior to the Council. It is my hope that this book will help those who have struggled to understand the roots of the crisis and encourage them to place greater trust in and fidelity to the Magisterium for the sake of unity in the Church.

— Fr. Matthew Mary Bartow, MFVA
Assistant Chaplain at EWTN

With *Ignorance of Things Divine*, Andrew Mioni offers a valuable perspective for navigating through the difficult realities in the world and in the Church. His insightful, historical outlook illustrates how division, controversy, contention, and confusion within the Church is nothing new, but also how it is always the Church herself who wisely offers the correct solutions to Her own problems and to the problems of the world in which She operates. With honorable deference and respect for the Church, Mr. Mioni also sheds light on how disrespect and disregard for the authority of the Church in whatever day or age ultimately is what gives birth to crises and erodes one's very own faith. *Ignorance of Things Divine* is a well-composed and well-documented reminder of our need to listen to and trust in the guidance of the

Popes and the Magisterium; it is also an implicit warning of the need to turn a deaf ear to dissenters both inside and outside the Church's walls. In the end, echoing Our Lord's humble obedience, His life of merciful and self-giving charity, and embracing the Church's call to holiness are the solution to whatever crisis we face in our day.

— Fr. Terrance J.M. Chartier, S.T.B.
Host at Mother of the Redeemer Retreat
Center, Bloomington, IN

Ignorance of Things Divine is more than just a masterful survey of the landscape behind "traditionalism"; for me, it's personal. For a number of years, having absorbed - uncritically - the usual traditionalist talking points about Vatican II and the Novus Ordo, I was beyond convinced that these constituted the crux of the crisis in the Catholic Church. If we could only return to the "Mass of the Ages" and jettison the ambiguities (or heresies!) of the Second Vatican Council, we would restore the Church to her Tridentine glory, and parishes would be bursting with well-catechized, young families. Andrew's book is unique in that, not only does it deconstruct and correct this narrative by identifying the preconciliar roots of this crisis, it does so using a source that all sides can agree on: the Magisterium itself. Had *Ignorance of Things Divine* been written earlier, it would have rescued me from the clutches of radical traditionalism, and saved me years of needless despair and anger. Better late than never.

— Dustin Quick
Host of *Holy Smokes:
Cigars, Catholicism, and Conversation*

Andrew Mioni's *Ignorance of Things Divine* is both a thoughtful and timely achievement. The crises of our age are no secret among the perplexed faithful. The growing sentiments of empiricism (denial of the supernatural), materialism (pursuit of earthly goods), religious indifferentism (denial of objective spiritual truth), apathy, and nominal Catholicism are more present than ever. These scandals, while addressed by both Vatican I and Vatican II, have served to ostracize many, and it is the purpose of this work to diagnose our modern time without recourse to shallow reactionism, but by highlighting the thorough response of Holy Mother Church and offering this most urgent advice for navigating the tensions of our post-conciliar discourse. Too many have pointed the finger at the hierarchy - even going so far as to blame the achievements of the Second Vatican Council - using it a kind of scapegoat - for the hindrance of unity and clarity. However, Mioni's treatment on such subjects as religious liberty, the authority of the Magisterium, and evangelization provides a remedy for the too-common romanticized nostalgia of the "pre-conciliar" Church and the unfiltered vilification of the present. In these nine chapters, he demonstrates that, at the heart of it all, the Church has identified the root cause as a crisis of authority - a contempt for the authority which has been divinely established for our benefit. It is my hope, as an apologist and OCIA instructor, to thoroughly integrate these clear prescriptions: the call of obedience to the Church's Magisterium, fidelity to what God has revealed, holiness in both our personal lives and in community, and the missionary zeal which we find demonstrated by so many of our saints. This work is not a mere critique of our modern times nor the common reactions to it. Rather, it serves as a guide, bolstered by the wisdom of the Church, to restore holy, convicted influence to our secular age. I wholeheartedly commend this work to all catechists, apologists, theologians, and to any Catholic who wishes to find guidance from the Magisterium for the aforementioned diagnosis of our modern age towards spiritual renewal.

— Brayden Cook
Catholic Apologist and OCIA Instructor
Host of *The Catechumen*

Ignorance of Things Divine

The True Crisis of Faith –
And Its Remedy –
According to the Magisterium

Andrew Mioni

En Route Books and Media, LLC
Saint Louis, MO

En Route Books and Media, LLC
5705 Rhodes Avenue
St. Louis, MO 63109

Contact us at **contactus@enroutebooksandmedia.com**

Cover Credit: Andrew Mioni, using Hugo van der Goes' "The Fall of Man and the Lamentation," at picryl.com

Copyright © 2026 Andrew Mioni

ISBN-13: 979-8-88870-498-1
Library of Congress Control Number:
Available online at https://catalog.loc.gov

Scripture passages taken from the Revised Standard Version – Catholic Edition (RSV-CE). *Emphases added unless otherwise noted.*

All rights reserved. No part of this book may be reproduced, stored in a retrieval system, or transmitted in any form, or by any means, electronic, mechanical, photocopying, or otherwise, without the prior written permission of the author.

The enemy has, indeed, long been prowling about the fold and attacking it with such subtle cunning that now, more than ever before, the prediction of the Apostle to the elders of the Church of Ephesus seems to be verified: "I know that . . . fierce wolves will get in among you, and will not spare the flock." Those who still are zealous for the glory of God are seeking the causes and reasons for this decline in religion. Coming to a different explanation, each points out, according to his own view, a different plan for the protection and restoration of the kingdom of God on earth. But it seems to Us, Venerable Brethren, that while we should not overlook other considerations, We are forced to agree with those who hold that the chief cause of the present indifference and, as it were, infirmity of soul, and the serious evils that result from it, is to be found above all in ignorance of things divine. This is fully in accord with what God Himself declared through the Prophet Osee: "And there is no knowledge of God in the land."

- *Pope St. Pius X, "Acerbo Nimis" (1905)*

Also from Andrew Mioni

Altar Against Altar: An Analysis of Catholic Traditionalism

Contributor:

Faith in Crisis: Critical Dialogues in Catholic Traditionalism, Church Authority, and Reform

My Grandpa, The Pope: From Sedevacantist Sect to the Catholic Church - A Memoir

To Pope Leo XIII,
from whom I learned so much in the course of my research for this book.

And to our new Supreme Pontiff, Pope Leo XIV.
May he guide the Church through the storm of our time with all the wisdom and clarity of his predecessors.

Table of Contents

Testimonials i

Acknowledgments xv

Foreword xvii

Introduction 1

Chapter 1: The Roots of the Crisis 13

Chapter 2: Religious Indifferentism 25

Chapter 3: Naturalism 35

Chapter 4: Materialism 57

Chapter 5: Catholics in Name Only 73

Chapter 6: A New Era 89

Chapter 7: The True Source of the Crisis 109

Chapter 8: Toward a Solution 133

Chapter 9: Salt and Light 149

Acknowledgments

First and foremost, I want to thank my beautiful wife Clelia for her patience and encouragement as I took on the challenge of writing another book during a flurry of activities in our home life. Knowing as she does that writing and publishing books has been a lifelong dream of mine, her support is central to these endeavors, and I am very grateful.

I would also like to thank everyone who took the time to read the book in advance and provide a testimonial. Their words of support and recommendation are most appreciated.

A special thanks goes to Dave Armstrong for his generosity in providing the foreword. Dave's work has been instrumental on me over the years in navigating this and other similar topics, and I am very thankful for his willingness to contribute to this book.

I also would like to extend my gratitude to those who operate the site Papal Encyclicals Online, for maintaining such an excellent database of documents and providing an easy resource to use.

Foreword

Andrew Mioni is currently one of the most brilliant orthodox Catholic analysts of the ongoing controversies regarding the "traditionalist" wing of the Catholic Church and its troublesome radical offshoots, and the "roots" behind the current, very real crisis in the Church: one that no one denies. His superb book, *Altar Against Altar: An Analysis of Catholic Traditionalism* (En Route Books & Media, June 2024) was filled to the brim with helpful insights and hopeful solutions.

In this volume, he specifically refutes the simplistic and rather absurd allegation that the Second Vatican Council (1962-1965) was the primary cause of various serious difficulties and problems in the Catholic Church today. Historical causation (especially in matters of theology) is, however, always far more complex than that. Mioni notes Pope St. Pius X's warning over a century ago that Modernism was "present almost in the very veins and heart of the Church" (*Pascendi Dominici Gregis*, 1907). This was not merely dissent from the Catholic Church *outside* her fold. It was already a serious problem *inside* the

Church, indeed in her very "heart" according to this saint-pope and scourge of Modernism, particularly beloved by traditionalists and more radical reactionary Catholics.

In light of statements of that sort, we must go much further back and deeper into history to properly understand the destructive phenomenon that confronts us today, and Mioni conveniently provides the resources and framework to do this necessary work. In his Introduction he stresses the obvious but so often neglected starting point of any such analysis: "I consulted the writings of the Magisterium and listened to what Holy Mother Church had said in her wisdom." Amen! Back to basics . . .

The 18th century was a time of growing theological liberalism and rejection of existing Catholic tradition. Hence, Mioni cites Pope Pius VI's 1775 encyclical *Inscrutabile Divinae Sapientiae*, where he stated that it was "a time when many plots are laid against orthodox religion" and that "confusion is spread wide by men maddened by a monstrous desire of innovation." *That* has a familiar ring, doesn't it?

It sounds like our own time because there have *always* been problems of heterodoxy and possible schism in the Church, *from the beginning*, as proven by St. Paul's many scathing condemnations of divisiveness and lack of theological unity among the earliest Christians, in his epistles. Jesus thought it important enough to pray during the Last Supper for His disciples, and by extension, *all* of His followers throughout history, "that they may be one *even as we are one*, I in them and thou in me, that they may become *perfectly one*, so that the world may know that thou hast sent me" (Jn 17:22-23, RSV). At every turn, then, we find these problems, and this is what the book addresses, concentrating on more recent centuries. Mioni hits the nail on the head in his Chapter Three:

> Thus it is clear that Modernism is rooted in the same errors that had been infecting the world; namely, a denial of revelation and an exclusion of God to make way for human reason. Naturally, the Modernist's doctrines support the concept of religious indifferentism as well. As Pius X further wrote, "*Indeed*

> *Modernists do not deny but actually admit, some confusedly, others in the most open manner, that all religions are true..."*

These are compelling words from Pope Pius X, and should demonstrate beyond any doubt that this crisis of faith had already taken deep root in the world many years before Vatican II. [his italics; citation from *Pascendi Dominici Gregis*]

We mustn't neglect the role of social media, either, in spreading morally and spiritually harmful material and false notions. Like all technologies and media, it can be used for great good (I have sought to do that, myself, these past 28 years) or great evil. Mioni cites Venerable Pope Pius XII in his encyclical *Miranda Prorsus* from 1957, where he virtually predicted the Internet and its huge ramifications in society:

> Today the mounting technological advances in communicating pictures, sounds, and ideas must be subjected to the sweet yoke of the law of Christ if they are not to become

> a source of countless evils… here the issue is not real freedom, … but unchecked license to express oneself without regard for prudence, even though this be contrary to sound morals and liable to result in serious danger for souls.

Andrew Mioni helpfully documents from many popes, things that we foolishly think are either *confined solely* to our own age, or *worse* at present than they have ever been. Pope Leo XIII in *Sapientiae Christianae* (1890) referred to "the inertness and internal dissensions of Catholics" that "have contributed to the present condition of things." In his encyclical, *Octobri Mense* (1891), he also lamented "that so many Catholics should be such in name only, and should pay to religion no honor or worship." And Pope Pius XI echoed this opinion in *Divini Redemptoris* (1937): "Even in Catholic countries there are still too many who are Catholics hardly more than in name…We know how much Our Divine Savior detested this empty pharisaic show…"

As King Solomon observed almost 3,000 years ago in Ecclesiastes 1:9: "what has been done is what will be done; and there is nothing new under the sun." Philosopher George Santayana expressed a somewhat similar notion in his famous words from 1905, "Those who cannot remember the past are condemned to repeat it." There were, indeed, relative "golden ages" in Church history, but assuredly they were never totally free of problems much like the ones we are plagued with today. The Catholic Church has always been in need of reform at all times (*ecclesia semper reformanda est* – as we say in Latin).

In his Chapter Seven, "The True Source of the Crisis," Mioni documents how Pope Leo XII identified "the true source of all the evils" as "a dogged contempt for the Church's authority" (*Ubi Primum*, 1824). Likewise, Pope Leo XIII believed that "the source of these evils lies chiefly . . . in this, that the holy and venerable authority of the Church, . . . has been despised and set aside" (*Inscrutabili Dei Consilio*, 1878). One might argue – and Mioni does – that this, along with a rejection of the full inspiration of the Bible, lies at the root of the premises behind Modernism and theological liberalism.

I fully agree with what Mioni asserted in the same chapter: "It is not that Vatican II *caused* the crisis, but that it *revealed* a crisis which had been simmering for centuries, . . . the popes had been warning the world for many years about it." And also, "The fact that these evils came to light *after* the Council does not mean they came *because* of the Council." The old logical fallacy, *post hoc, ergo propter hoc* (Latin for "after this, therefore because of this") is as profoundly relevant today as it has always been. Making Vatican II the big bad boogeyman for every bad thing is a classic case of this type of illogical, shoddy thinking.

We see, clearly, then, that problems supposedly solely or primarily brought about by Vatican II are simply those that have always been present in the Church and in human hearts and souls, and are essentially identical to the sins and prominent strains of philosophical or nominal unbelief and lack of piety and virtue that run through all societies and religious groups and virtually all human beings at all times. Andrew Mioni's book is crucial reading that will help any reader – particularly Catholic ones – become aware of what popes have authoritatively stated about these matters, and to have a much better grasp of the sources and background of present-day difficulties within the Catholic Church and by extension, the wider world.

Dave Armstrong

Author of *Reflections on Radical Catholic Reactionaries* (2002; rev. 2013 and 2023) and *Mass Movements: Radical Catholic Reactionaries, the New Mass, and Ecumenism* (2012)

Introduction

Many Catholics today speak of a crisis in the Church. They speak of a crisis of faith, as evidenced by empty pews, a general disinterest in religion, and a display of spiritual apathy in the face of the distractions and comforts of the world. They speak of a crisis of the liturgy, as can be seen in casual, irreverent, and even sometimes sacrilegious offerings of the Sacrifice of the Mass. They speak of a vocations crisis, displayed by low numbers of men entering seminaries and women entering religious life. It can hardly be disputed that a spiritual crisis afflicts the Church and has for some time.

This crisis is often discussed in tandem with the Second Vatican Council and its reforms. The Council met from 1962 to 1965, with the intention of establishing a strategy for the Church to confront the challenges of the modern age, but was immediately followed by confusion and chaos. Many lay faithful did not have a clear understanding of why the Council was called or what it taught, and in the aftermath, it was often difficult to discern authentic conciliar teaching from liberties taken in the name of the

Council. The revolutionary spirit of the decade, mingled with the vague notion that the Council had intended to "update" certain practices or teachings, led many clergy and lay people alike to act according to the "spirit of Vatican II", as it came to be known; a spirit of change and of discarding the past. Long-standing practices became neglected, traditional teachings were spurned, and the influence of a very secularized world seemed to hold much more sway than spiritual conviction.

After attempting to navigate the chaos in the years following Vatican II, a subset of Catholics came to believe that the Council itself had introduced this crisis of faith into the Church. It seemed to them that the heresy of Modernism, condemned in the early 20th century by Pope St. Pius X, had infiltrated the Church and spread to the upper echelons of the hierarchy, taking root over the next several decades until the Holy See itself was infected by this heresy's errors. Vatican II appeared to be proof of this, as the years before the Council saw a Church in its stately glory, while the years that followed were marred by doctrinal, liturgical, and catechetical disorder. Vatican II had intended to bring the Church out into the world, but it appeared as though the opposite had occurred. This subset of Catholics believed that the Council was either ambiguous in its declarations at best, or nefarious in its intentions at worst, and attempted to compromise Catholic teaching by diluting or even contradicting current doctrine. These Catholics believed that a return to the "traditional", pre-Vatican II ways would restore order in the Church, and thus they became known as the "traditionalists."

Catholic traditionalism has since generated a movement of resistance built around the crisis. While some groups were reconciled to the Church after formally accepting the Council (such as the Priestly Fraternity of St. Peter, or FSSP), others cited this crisis as a justification for establishing a ministry separate from the Church's juridical structure, and set about building chapels, communities, and religious orders that followed the pre-conciliar ways, which they saw as "necessary for the reconstruction of the Church."[1] (Believing that the formation of priests and bishops is done under the erroneous

---

[1] Marcel Lefebvre, "1988 Episcopal Consecrations sermon," SSPX website. https://sspx.org/en/1988-episcopal-consecrations-sermon-of-archbishop-lefebvre

principles of Vatican II, and the Church's hierarchy is established according to the Council's vision, they view it necessary to operate independently of them until Vatican II simply fades into obscurity as a failed experiment, while trusting that the traditional ways will continue to attract followers until they eventually become the majority).

Much of their published material is centered around this idea of the crisis in the Church. For example, the SSPX, or Society of St. Pius X (the largest independent traditionalist group) has created the "Crisis in the Church Series" which explains, among other things, their stance on the Council and other traditionalist groups, and why they believe an independent ministry is justified in order to fight this crisis. Other organizations such as the news outlet *Crisis Magazine* lend their voices to championing traditionalism, as well as public figures and authors affiliated with this movement.

Having been raised in various traditionalist circles, I have had to engage with the crisis narrative for many years. And while I can certainly agree that there is a crisis of faith today, it has always seemed to me that the traditionalists' stance is rather inconclusive, and seems to generate more questions than answers. There is one decisive question I have researched for some time that I believe is crucial to this conversation. And that question is: when will this crisis end?[2]

Surely wherever one finds themselves in this debate, all can agree that the Church cannot exist in an indefinite state of crisis. That is far too pessimistic an outlook for a Catholic to have. The Church is the Bride of Christ, the "pillar and foundation of truth" (1 Timothy 3:15), birthed at Pentecost and existing for thousands of years through persecution, war, and every sort of evil that can befall humanity. And yet we are to believe a crisis unlike any other came about within the last 60 years or so? Clearly this crisis did not exist at one point in the recent past, and it surely will not exist at some point in the future. What has occurred in this time that the Church has never faced before? Should we not try to diagnose this crisis and find out exactly what needs to be done to remedy it?

---

[2] For a more extensive exploration of this question, see Mioni, *Altar Against Altar: An Analysis of Catholic Traditionalism,* Chapter 12

Is it merely a question of redacting Vatican II from the history books? Most Catholics have never even read the documents of Vatican II, and many things done in the name of Vatican II were not even called for by the Council (as the traditionalists will agree). They came as a result of an independent spirit, disregard of authority, and abuse of power. An example of this can be seen in the experimentation with matter other than bread and wine for Mass— a practice that, it should be obvious, was never once discussed at Vatican II. Even accepting the traditionalists' stance that Vatican II planted this crisis within the Church, do we expect that it would simply disappear as soon as the Council was redacted? The Church would still be faced with all the challenges of modernity that continue to devastate supernatural faith.

Must we look back further, and lay the blame on Modernism? This seems just as inconclusive. As Pope St. Pius X made clear, Modernism had spread to such an extensive degree that it had entered the very heart of the Church by the early 20th century (as he wrote, "[T]he most pernicious of all the adversaries of the Church…put into operation their designs for her undoing, not from without but from within. Hence, the danger is present almost in the very veins and heart of the Church, whose injury is the more certain from the very fact that their knowledge of her is more intimate."[3]). If a heresy was so prevalent that the Church's attempts at purging it were unsuccessful, how was it allowed to reach this point in the first place?

And who has the authority to determine when and how this crisis ends? From whom did they receive the authority to make this determination? If one traditionalist group thinks it has ended, but another thinks it has not, which is correct? And if one group believes it has ended, is it not ultimately up to each individual person who follows that group to decide if that decision is correct, thereby demonstrating that this is ultimately a matter of private judgment?

Unless we know how these errors came to be and how they were allowed to spread, we cannot get to the root of the problem. But this crisis is certainly not something that can be measured in polls or tallies, or

---

[3] Pius X, *Pascendi Dominici Gregis* (1907). https://papalencyclicals.net/pius10/p10pasce.htm

can simply become a non-issue once a certain numeric threshold is reached, like the percentage of Catholics who believe in the Real Presence in the Eucharist or who regularly attend Sunday Mass. Our faith is not something measurable or quantifiable, and neither is the cause of its weakness or absence.

These are questions that need answers; answers I was determined to learn. In the words of Pope Pius XI, "For anyone who, as We do, desires profoundly to study and successfully to apply the means necessary to overcome such evils, it is all-important that he recognize both the fact and the gravity of this state of affairs and attempt beforehand to discover its causes."[4] But this is a subject that has long occupied those much more knowledgeable than I, and can be explored through the lens of history, philosophy, theology, and politics (as the SSPX even admits[5]). So I proceeded to do what every Catholic layman can and should do; I consulted the writings of the Magisterium and listened to what Holy Mother Church had

---

[4] Pius XI, *Ubi Arcano Dei Consilio* (1922). https://papalencyclicals.net/pius11/p11arcan.htm

[5] "The crisis: problems, causes, remedies," SSPX website. https://sspx.org/en/crisis-problems-causes-remedies

said in her wisdom. Whether one styles oneself a "traditionalist" or not, Catholics can agree that the writings of the supreme authority to which we are all subject are reliable sources.

In my research through the papal archives to identify the source of this crisis, I discovered that the Magisterium had been consistently ringing the alarm bells on a crisis that was infecting the Church long before the 1960s. It was indeed too simple to point to certain heresies or groups, not to mention that it attributes levels of power and influence to them which are miniscule in comparison to the power of Christ's Church. (In answer to those who see Freemasonry as the cause, as some do, we might look to Pope Leo XIII, who wrote, "We do not wish to exaggerate the masonic power by attributing to its direct and immediate action all the evils which presently preoccupy Us."[6]) Error had compounded on error over the centuries to create a threat to supernatural faith that infected public and private life, driving God from the

---

[6] Leo XIII, *Custodi Di Quella Fede* (1892). https://papalencyclicals.net/leo13/ l13ms3.htm

hearts and minds of the faithful. The root of this crisis, as I discovered, was much broader and much older. And it is that which I intend to share here.

I do not intend for this book to be completely comprehensive in its analysis of the crisis, nor absolutely definitive in its conclusions. This is not an exhaustive list of every encyclical or document that addresses this issue; I have simply included the ones I found clear and helpful in my research. There are too many factors for any single book or author to consolidate. I simply hope to provide greater context for this crisis of faith with sources that all Catholics can agree are authoritative, and to present the case that this crisis has much deeper and older roots than those which are usually identified.

My hope is for this book to provide some common ground that can further these discussions, so that the conversation around this topic can advance beyond simplistic analyses. Traditionalism and its associated beliefs about the crisis in the Church have spread far and wide, especially in the age of the internet and social media, and it is my belief that this subject ought to be given more extensive discussion and investigation. An unfortunate rift has developed in the wake of Vatican II, one that pits those who adhere to traditionalism against those who have accepted the reforms of the Council, creating factions and disagreements that often do more to perpetuate divisions in the Church than heal them. This is especially relevant because of the multitude of converts coming into the Church, who may be discouraged by seeing such a sharp divide. Or, being new members of the Church, they may not have studied the nuances and history behind the issue and might be led into believing that the Church they joined may not be all they thought it was.

My objective is not to dispute the traditionalists' claims of a crisis, nor even to dispute the very real seriousness of it. My objective is to demonstrate that once we dig further and follow the roots all the way down, we come to a source that is much broader. What I hope to do in this book is to shed light on the true source of this crisis, which the Church identified long ago, and to point to a remedy that all can agree on as a pathway forward. The Magisterium has provided a roadmap, and although its descriptions are dire, we may be confident that they will provide direction for uprooting this crisis. To use the words of

Pope Pius XI from his 1922 encyclical *Ubi Arcano Dei Consilio,* "Up to this We have analyzed briefly the causes of the ills which afflict present-day society, the recital of which however, ...should not cause us to lose hope of finding their appropriate remedy, since the evils themselves seem to suggest a way out of these difficulties."[7] Let us proceed with examining the roots of this crisis, so that despite its tragic influence and spread, it may provide us with answers to the questions: when and how did this crisis begin, and when and how will it end?

---

[7] Pius XI, *Ubi Arcano Dei Consilio.* https://papalencyclicals.net/pius11/p11arcan.htm

Chapter 1

The Roots of the Crisis

Do thou, O Lord, protect us, guard us ever from this generation. On every side the wicked prowl, as vileness is exalted among the sons of men. (Ps 12:7-8)

It is my opinion that the third session of the First Vatican Council provides a clear explanation for how this crisis came to develop. Vatican I was convened in 1869 and ended the next year. This Council had the benefit of hindsight in surveying the aftermath of the Council of Trent and took place at a time in which the world had vastly advanced in terms of technology, travel, industry, and global change. Its decrees are confirmed by the encyclicals in the century preceding it, and in reapplying its diagnosis of the conditions of its time to the century that followed (a century which ended right around the time of Vatican II), it is quite apparent that these seeds of the crisis continued to grow, despite the various attempts to curb them in the form of repeated papal denunciations, the Syllabus of Errors, forceful attempts at the purgation of Modernism, and so forth.

We will use sections 4 through 8 of its third session as the roadmap for navigating this crisis. To begin, we will look at sections 4 through 6, dedicating several chapters to the circumstances (and the results of them) that they describe. These three sections read as follows:

> 4. While we recall with grateful hearts, as is only fitting, [the] outstanding gains, which the divine mercy has bestowed on the church especially by means of [the Council of Trent], we cannot subdue the bitter grief that we feel at most serious evils, which have largely arisen either because the authority of the sacred synod was held in contempt by all too many, or because its wise decrees were neglected.

> 5. Everybody knows that those heresies, condemned by the fathers of Trent, which rejected the divine magisterium of the Church

and allowed religious questions to be a matter for the judgment of each individual, have gradually collapsed into a multiplicity of sects, either at variance or in agreement with one another; and by this means a good many people have had all faith in Christ destroyed.

6. Indeed even the Holy Bible itself, which they at one time claimed to be the sole source and judge of the Christian faith, is no longer held to be divine, but they begin to assimilate it to the inventions of myth.[8]

Considering these three points (rejection of authority, private judgment, and the reduction of the word of God to the "word of man"), let us proceed with examining several encyclicals that provide descriptions of the time after the Council of Trent.

The following passage from Pope Clement XIII's 1761 encyclical *In Dominico Agro*, describing the aftermath of the Council, may demonstrate that the chaos following Vatican II is not unprecedented; this

---

[8] "First Vatican Council." EWTN, https://ewtn.com/catholicism/library/first-vatican-council-1505

describes the Church's current plight in the 21st century almost exactly!

> Agreement on a method of teaching was almost destroyed, and the weak members of the faithful were scandalized at finding that they were no longer united by the same language and topics. On the other hand, contentions arose from different ways of transmitting Catholic truth and disunity of spirit and great disagreements from rivalry while one declared he was a follower of Apollo, another of Cephas, and another of Paul [1 Cor 1:12]. We think that nothing can be more fatal to God's greater glory than the bitterness of those disagreements. Nothing can eliminate more disastrously the fruits which the faithful should gain from Christian discipline.

> Thus it is necessary to have the salt of wisdom to preserve the love of neighbor and to offset weaknesses. If they turn from zeal for wisdom and from concern for their neighbor to disagreement, they have salt without

peace—not a gift of virtue but a cause for condemnation. [...] We pray to God in affliction of spirit and in humility of heart to bestow his indulgence and mercy on our efforts to prevent disagreement disturbing the faithful, and to ensure that in the bond of peace and charity of spirit, we all know, praise, and glorify the one God and our Lord Jesus Christ[.][9]

Rejecting the guiding voice of the Church, especially with regard to the Catechism that was meant to clarify Catholic teaching, individuals attempted to navigate the post-conciliar confusion on their own at a time when the Church was beset by heterodox beliefs. How much more did people need an absolute authority in those days! And yet they "held in contempt" or "neglected" the decrees of the Council which intended to provide a pathway out of the spiritual darkness.

We can next turn to Pope Leo XII's *Ubi Primum*, who had issued a warning about liberties taken with the Bible against ecclesiastical authority. The various

---

[9] Clement XIII, *In Dominico Agro* (1761). https://papalencyclicals.net/clem13/ c13indom.htm

Protestant sects had reduced the authority of the Church to the Bible alone, but naturally, with a myriad of translations and interpretations and no magisterial authority to settle these debates, chaos ensued. Leo XII warned against those who "try to turn against religion the sacred writings divinely given to us for the building up of religion" by "[r]ejecting the traditions of the holy Fathers and infringing the well-known decree of the Council of Trent" and producing their own translations with faulty commentaries and interpretations that became "a gospel of men, or what is worse, a gospel of the devil!"[10]

The next pope, Pius VIII, also spoke about the confusion that had come about from personal interpretations of the Bible during this time, in his encyclical *Traditi Humilitati*:

> We must also be wary of those who publish the Bible with new interpretations contrary to the Church's laws. [...] The sacred Synod of Trent had decreed in order to restrain impudent characters, that no one, relying on his

---

[10] Leo XII, *Ubi Primum* (1824). https://papalencyclicals.net/leo12/ l12ubipr.htm

own prudence in matters of faith and of conduct which concerns Christian doctrine, might twist the sacred Scriptures to his own opinion, or to an opinion contrary to that of the Church or the popes. Though such machinations against the Catholic faith had been assailed long ago by these canonical proscriptions, Our recent predecessors made a special effort to check these spreading evils.[11]

As the Magisterium confirmed, rejection of ecclesiastical authority devolved into private judgment and sectarianism, leading to disunity and dissensions in the Church among groups that each claimed to have the fullness of truth. And as Vatican I indicated, once the ultimate authority was removed and religious questions became no more than subjective opinions, even the Bible itself was no longer seen as divinely revealed truth, but merely as teachings handed down from a human source.

Where does this bring us? Before the turn of the 19th century, Pope Pius VI provides a clear picture

---

[11] Pius VIII, *Traditi Humilitati* (1829). https://papalencyclicals.net/pius08/ p8tradit.htm

of the challenges the Church faced. In his 1775 encyclical *Inscrutabile*, he wrote the following:[12]

> Who would not be fearful at the present condition of the Christian people? [...] Who would not be shocked when considering that We have undertaken the task of guarding and protecting the Church at a time when many plots are laid against orthodox religion, when the safe guidance of the sacred canons is rashly despised, and when confusion is spread wide by men maddened by a monstrous desire of innovation, who attack the very bases of rational nature and attempt to overthrow them?

One might reasonably guess that this quote came from one of the pontiffs of the mid-20th century. It certainly describes the plight of the Church for the last several decades accurately. In that time, individuals who have nefarious intentions toward the Church have made no secret of this fact. There has

---

[12] Pius VI, *Inscrutabile* (1775). https://papalencyclicals.net/pius06/p6inscru.htm

Chapter 1: The Roots of the Crisis

been wanton disregard for disciplinary norms, and those who claim the Church's teachings are outdated or irrelevant to modern man are very vocal. But as Pius VI shows, the Church had been facing these problems long before Vatican II.

Pius VI's *Inscrutabile* continues as follows:

> We refer to the pestilent disease which the wickedness of our times brings forth. We must unite our minds and strength in treating this plague before it grows rife and becomes incurable in the Church through Our oversight.
>
> *[Men] have come to such a height of impiety that they make out that God does not exist, or if He does that He is idle and uncaring, making no revelation to men.* Consequently it is not surprising that they assert that everything holy and divine is the product of the minds of inexperienced men smitten with empty fear of the future and seduced by a vain hope of immortality.
>
> When they have spread this darkness abroad and torn religion out of men's hearts,

these accursed philosophers proceed to destroy the bonds of union among men, both those which unite them to their rulers, and those which urge them to their duty. They keep proclaiming that man is born free and subject to no one, that society accordingly is a crowd of foolish men who stupidly yield to priests who deceive them and to kings who oppress them, so that the harmony of priest and ruler is only a monstrous conspiracy against the innate liberty of man.

They cause a serious loss of souls redeemed by Christ's blood wherever their teaching spreads, like a cancer; it forces its way into public academies, into the houses of the great, into the palaces of kings, *and even enters the sanctuary, shocking as it is to say so.*

The affair is of the greatest importance since it concerns the Catholic faith, the purity of the Church, the teaching of the saints, the peace of the empire, and the safety of nations.[13]

---

[13] Ibid.

There are several connections to be noted here. The first and most obvious is the gravity of the situation. It is clear that Pius VI is not referring to a problem which has just begun to rear its head. This had been growing for some time. As Pius VI notes, rejection of God and denial of revelation led to proclaiming a supposed liberty from all forms of authority. And this was spreading throughout public associations and even into the Church itself.

Pius VI provides a crucial connection in this encyclical. In casting off religious authority, those who rebelled against the Church had followed the natural trajectory toward concluding that divine revelation is nonexistent, and therefore any religious interpretation or teaching may very well have equal merit. As Pope Leo XIII would write many years later, those who, "trusting in their turn to their own way of thinking…deny that there is any such thing as revelation or inspiration" are the "true children and inheritors of the older heretics" who "[relied] on private judgment and [repudiated] the divine traditions and teaching office of the Church."[14] This brings our

---

[14] Leo XIII, *Providentissimus Deus* (1893). https://papalencyclicals.net/leo13/l13provi.htm

examination of the crisis to its next facet— the error of religious indifferentism.

Chapter 2

Religious Indifferentism

*Those who choose another god
multiply their sorrows[.] (Ps 16:4)*

Like any aspect of this crisis of faith, religious indifferentism could not have developed in a vacuum. Reeling from the divisions around the time of Trent, and having its authority challenged on an unprecedented scale, the Church found herself in a precarious situation. Her display of authority in the form of anathemas and decrees may have internally re-established order and rectified the various abuses that were occurring, but when faced with a "multiplicity of sects" that had long since cast off the Church's authority, these condemnations landed on stony ground. What good is an authoritative decree if those it is leveled at do not believe there is any authority issuing it? And so while the Church worked to resolve the internal errors that had compounded, codifying the liturgy and re-establishing ecclesiastical discipline, the storm raged on outside her walls.

Returning to Pope Leo XII's *Ubi Primum*, issued in 1824, we can see an explicit connection between private judgment and religious indifferentism. Lamenting the "fierce and mighty conflicts which have raged in Our times and continue to rage almost daily against the Catholic religion"[15], Leo XII wrote the following:

> A certain sect, which you surely know, has unjustly arrogated to itself the name of philosophy, and has aroused from the ashes the disorderly ranks of practically every error. Under the gentle appearance of piety and liberality this sect professes what they call tolerance or indifferentism. *It preaches that…in religion, God has given every individual a wide freedom to embrace and adopt without danger to his salvation whatever sect or opinion appeals to him on the basis of his private judgment.*
>
> Of course this error is not new, but in Our days it rages with a new rashness against the

---

[15] Leo XII, *Ubi Primum* (1824). https://papalencyclicals.net/leo12/l12ubipr.htm

> constancy and integrity of the Catholic faith. [...] *The current indifferentism has developed to the point of arguing that everyone is on the right road. This includes not only all those sects which though outside the Catholic Church verbally accept revelation as a foundation, but those groups too which spurn the idea of divine revelation and profess a pure deism or even a pure naturalism.*[16]

Leo XII went on to explain that the central error lies in the fact that religious indifferentism denies the truth about God, or rather, that it denies objective truth itself, since God *is* truth. As Leo XII further wrote, "It is impossible for the most true God, who is Truth Itself, the best, the wisest Provider, and the Rewarder of good men, to approve all sects who profess false teachings which are often inconsistent with one another and contradictory, and to confer eternal rewards on their members."[17] If all religions are equally true, then truth is not absolute and cannot be binding

---

[16] Ibid.
[17] Ibid.

on anyone, because any variety of opinions or teachings all have equal value. This erodes all sense of divine authority because without truth, there is no authority. If God "makes no revelation to man", in the words of Pius VI from *Inscrutabile*, then religion is not something given to us from without, but something we develop from within, meaning any interpretation of it is equally valid.

It is important to note that, in his condemnation of religious indifferentism, Leo XII calls attention to the fact that it developed from indifference of *opinion*. There is a natural progression from private judgment to religious indifferentism, although it may manifest in different degrees. If there is no ultimate authority, and each individual can decide not only what opinions or teachings are true but also that they can lead to salvation apart from (and even opposed to) the Church, there is no essential difference between one group and another, even if one denies belief in God altogether.

Returning also to Pius VIII's *Traditi Humilitati* from 1829, we see the same errors identified. Pius VIII called attention to the "numberless errors and the teachings of perverse doctrines which, no longer secretly and clandestinely but openly and vigorously, attack the Catholic faith."[18] Of the state of society and the Church at the time, he writes:

> [T]he Roman See is assailed and the bonds of unity are, every day, being severed. The authority of the Church is weakened and the protectors of things sacred are snatched away and held in contempt. The holy precepts are despised, the celebration of divine offices is ridiculed, and the worship of God is cursed by the sinner. All things which concern religion are relegated to the fables of old women and the superstitions of priests. [...] [A]ll fear of religion has been lost, all discipline of morals has been abandoned, the sanctity of pure doctrine has been contested, and the rights of the sacred and of the civil powers have been trampled upon.[19]

---

[18] Pius VIII, *Traditi Humilitati* (1829). https://papalencyclicals.net/pius08/p8tradit.htm

[19] Ibid.

Even as long ago as the beginning of the 19th century, the Holy See knew that the challenges of the time were becoming a dire threat toward supernatural faith. Note that, just as Pius VI had warned of the world's ridicule toward that which is holy, Pius VIII over fifty years later also lamented the fact that religion had dwindled into fables and superstition. In this historical context of public contempt for the Church, Pius VIII issued his own warning of the errors of indifferentism:

> Among these heresies belongs that foul contrivance of the sophists of this age who do not admit any difference among the different professions of faith and who think that the portal of eternal salvation opens for all from any religion. They, therefore, label with the stigma of levity and stupidity those who, having abandoned the religion which they learned, embrace another of any kind, even Catholicism. This is certainly a monstrous impiety which assigns the same praise and the mark of the just and upright man to truth

and to error, to virtue and to vice, to goodness and to turpitude.[20]

The error of religious indifferentism had infected the world to such an extent by this time that the next pope, Gregory XVI, issued an encyclical specifically to address it, along with liberalism. In 1832, just a few short years after Pope Pius VIII had done so, Gregory XVI issued his own condemnation of this error in his encyclical *Mirari Vos*. He first provides the backdrop for this document, echoing his predecessors:

> Depravity exults; science is impudent; liberty, dissolute. The holiness of the sacred is despised; the majesty of divine worship is not only disapproved by evil men, but defiled and held up to ridicule. [...] The divine authority of the Church is opposed and her rights shorn off. She is subjected to human reason and with the greatest injustice exposed to the hatred of the people and reduced to vile servitude. The obedience due bishops is denied

---

[20] Ibid.

and their rights are trampled underfoot. Furthermore, academies and schools resound with new, monstrous opinions, which openly attack the Catholic faith; this horrible and nefarious war is openly and even publicly waged.[21]

In providing an analysis of indifferentism, he wrote that it is a "perverse opinion…spread on all sides by the fraud of the wicked who claim that *it is possible to obtain the eternal salvation of the soul by the profession of any kind of religion, as long as morality is maintained.*"[22] This, he wrote further, leads to the error of liberty of conscience, or "freedom of error", from which comes "transformation of minds, corruption of youths, contempt of sacred things and holy laws — in other words, a pestilence more deadly to the state than any other."[23]

---

[21] Gregory XVI, *Mirari Vos* (1832). https://papalencyclicals.net/greg16/g16mirar.htm
[22] Ibid.
[23] Ibid.

A pattern has started to emerge across these papal documents, one which sees a decline in respect for authority, especially divine authority, as both the cause and effect of religious indifferentism. Pope Bl. Pius IX, who condemned religious indifferentism on many occasions, also noted this connection. He stated in *Apostolicae Nostrae Caritatis* that "the sons of darkness, who are more artful than the sons of light…attempt to overthrow the authority of the Church's legitimate power and to corrupt the minds and souls of everyone" by spreading "the deadly virus of indifferentism and unbelief; to mix together all human and divine rights; to promote dissension, discord, and movements of impious rebellion[.]"[24] In *Singulari Quidem*, he called indifferentism one of the "deplorable evils which disturb and afflict both ecclesiastical and civil society", and that it "causes us to forget our duties to God…and…shakes almost to destruction the very basis of all law, justice and virtue."[25] In *Quanto Conficiamur Moerore*, he lamented the "corruption of morals

---

[24] Pius IX, *Apostolicae Nostrae Caritatis* (1854). https://papalencyclicals.net/pius09/p9aposto.htm

[25] Pius IX, *Singulari Quidem* (1856). https://papalencyclicals.net/pius09/p9singul.htm

so extensively increasing and promoted by...the deadly virus of unbelief and indifferentism spread far and wide; by contempt for ecclesiastical authority, sacred things, and laws...by the diabolical hatred of Christ, his Church, teaching, and of this Apostolic See."[26]

As we can see, the 19th century was already struggling under the weight of widespread error. Private judgment against the Church had over time given way to indifferentism, laying the foundation for a new error to afflict the Church. This denial of revelation, having simmered for many years, erupted under the papacy of Pope Pius IX, who spared no words in identifying and condemning this offspring of religious indifferentism— the error of naturalism.

---

[26] Pius IX, *Quanto Conficiamur Moerore* (1863). https://papalencyclicals.net/pius09/p9quanto.htm

Chapter 3

Naturalism

The kings of the earth set themselves, and the rulers take counsel together, against the LORD and his anointed, saying, "Let us burst their bonds asunder, and cast their cords from us." (Ps 2:2-3)

We now come to section 7 of Vatican I's third session, which describes the results of the turmoil that afflicted the Church as a result of private judgment and denial of revelation. The first half reads as follows:

> 7. Thereupon there came into being and spread far and wide throughout the world that doctrine of rationalism or naturalism,— utterly opposed to the Christian religion, since this is of supernatural origin,—which spares no effort to bring it about that Christ, who alone is our lord and savior, is shut out from the minds of people and the moral life

of nations. Thus they would establish what they call the rule of simple reason or nature.[27]

Let us first examine the connections between religious indifferentism and naturalism, and why one naturally leads to the other. (Recall that in 1824, Leo XII had written that religious indifferentism even favored the idea of salvation for those who reject divine revelation and adhere only to naturalism.)

Pope Bl. Pius IX drew the connection between these two errors in his encyclical *Quanta Cura*, a frequently-cited document in the context of the crisis in the Church. He defined naturalism as a system whose proponents demand that "human society be conducted and governed without regard being had to religion any more than if it did not exist; *or, at least, without any distinction being made between the true religion and false ones.*"[28] Pius IX unequivocally condemned naturalism in his *Syllabus of Errors*, along with pantheism and rationalism, the same errors he

---

[27] "First Vatican Council." EWTN, https://ewtn.com/catholicism/library/first-vatican-council-1505

[28] Pius IX, *Quanta Cura* (1864). https://papalencyclicals.net/pius09/p9quanta.htm

would list in Session 3 of Vatican I only several years later. In the *Syllabus*, he declared the following as propositions that were to be denounced: "All action of God upon man and the world is to be denied" and "divine revelation not only is not useful, but is even hurtful to the perfection of man."[29]

The denial of divine revelation that had crept into the Church and the world was finally rearing its head, and shedding any disguise of so-called "liberty" to display its true intent—a complete banishment of God from public life. Indifferentism may provide a semblance of personal autonomy, but on a large scale, if any opinion is equally meritorious, no system of belief is more worthy to be instituted as a form of governance than another. Therefore civil power is ultimately directed only by human reason, without any standard of morality to guide it.

Pope Pius IX's successor, Pope Leo XIII, provided a thorough explication of the connection between these two errors in his encyclical *Immortale Dei* from 1885. Citing the "harmful and deplorable

---

[29] Pius IX, *The Syllabus of Errors* (1864). https://papalencyclicals.net/pius09/p9syll.htm

passion for innovation which was aroused in the sixteenth century" as the source of "tenets of unbridled license...wildly conceived and boldly proclaimed as the principles and foundation of that new conception of law...at variance on many points with not only the Christian, but even the natural law"[30], he wrote:

> *The authority of God is passed over in silence, just as if there were no God; or as if He cared nothing for human society; or as if men, whether in their individual capacity or bound together in social relations, owed nothing to God; or as if there could be a government of which the whole origin and power and authority did not reside in God Himself.* Thus, as is evident, a State becomes nothing but a multitude which is its own master and ruler. And since the people is declared to contain within itself the spring-head of all rights and of all power, it follows that the State does not consider itself bound by any kind of duty toward God. Moreover, it believes that it is not

---

[30] Leo XIII, *Immortale Dei* (1885). https://papalencyclicals.net/leo13/l13sta.htm

obliged to make public profession of any religion; or to inquire which of the very many religions is the only one true; or to prefer one religion to all the rest; or to show to any form of religion special favor; but, on the contrary, is bound to grant equal rights to every creed, so that public order may not be disturbed by any particular form of religious belief.

And it is a part of this theory that all questions that concern religion are to be referred to private judgment; that every one is to be free to follow whatever religion he prefers, or none at all if he disapprove of all. From this the following consequences logically flow: that the judgment of each one's conscience is independent of all law; that the most unrestrained opinions may be openly expressed as to the practice or omission of divine worship; and that every one has unbounded license to think whatever he chooses and to publish abroad whatever he thinks.

Hence, lest concord be broken by rash charges, let this be understood by all, *that the integrity of Catholic faith cannot be reconciled with opinions verging on naturalism or rationalism, the essence of which is utterly to do away with Christian institutions and to install in society the supremacy of man to the exclusion of God.*[31]

Notably, this conclusion of naturalism mirrors what Pope Leo XIII also indicated was the objective of Freemasonry. As stated in the introduction, this book does not intend to provide a detailed analysis of this sect, but in the context of this chapter, it is a worthwhile aside to note that in *Inimica Vis*, Leo XIII wrote of the Masons: "They wish to see the religion founded by God repudiated and all affairs, private as well as public, regulated by the principles of naturalism alone; this is what, in their impiety and stupidity, they call the restoration of civil society."[32] He also wrote in *Custodi di Quella Fede*: "The facts say that in the plans of masonry, the names of political independence, equality, civilization, and progress aimed to facilitate the independence of man from God in

---

[31] Ibid.

[32] Leo XIII, *Inimica Vis (1892)*. https://papalencyclicals.net/leo13/l13ms4.htm

Chapter 3: Naturalism

our country. [...] It absolutely denies the supernatural, repudiating every revelation and all the means of salvation which revelation shows us."[33]

Pope Leo's somber warning about the effects of this error on society was timely. In 1888, only a few years after issuing *Immortale Dei*, he released his encyclical *Exeunte Iam Anno*, in which he stated the following:

> If We look into the kind of life men lead everywhere, it would be impossible to avoid the conclusion that public and private morals differ much from the precepts of the Gospel. Too sadly, alas, do the words of the Apostle St. John apply to our age, "all that is in the world, is the concupiscence of the flesh, and the concupiscence of the eyes and the pride of life."...Nor can We look to the future without fear, for new seeds of evil are sown, and as it were poured into the heart of the rising generation. [...] Many now-adays seek to learn by

---

[33] Leo XIII, *Custodi di Quella Fede* (1892). https://papalencyclicals.net/leo13/l13ms3.htm

the aid of reason alone, laying divine faith entirely aside; and, through the removal of its bright light, they stumble and fail to discern the truth, teaching for instance, that matter alone exists in the world; that men and beasts have the same origin and a like nature; there are some, indeed, who go so far as to doubt the existence of God, the Ruler and Maker of the World, or who err most grievously, like the heathens, as to the nature of God. Hence the very nature and form of virtue, justice, and duty are of necessity destroyed.

In this way We daily see the numerous ills which afflict all classes of men. *These poisonous doctrines have utterly corrupted both public and private life; rationalism, materialism, atheism, have begotten socialism, communism, nihilism—evil principles which it was not only fitting should have sprung from such parentage but were its necessary offspring.* [...] Hence the bonds of civil society will be utterly shattered when every man is driven by an unappeasable covetousness to a perpetual struggle, some striving to keep their possessions, others to obtain what they desire. *This is wellnigh the bent of our age.*[34]

A critical assessment of the world, indeed. Would the Church's warnings be heeded as the world rushed onward into a new century?

Pope St. Pius X, arguably the most often-cited pontiff in the struggle against this crisis of faith, was elected pope in 1903. Only two months into his pontificate, he issued his first encyclical, *E Supremi*, in which he presents no less bleak a situation than his predecessor:

> For who can fail to see that society is at the present time, more than in any past age, suffering from a terrible and deep-rooted malady which, developing every day and eating into its inmost being, is dragging it to destruction? You understand, Venerable Brethren, what this disease is — apostasy from God, than which in truth nothing is more allied with ruin, according to the word of the

---

[34] Leo XIII, *Exeunte Iam Anno* (1888). https://papalencyclicals.net/leo13/l13rgt.htm

Prophet: "For behold they that go far from Thee shall perish" (Ps. lxxii., 17).

[M]an has with infinite temerity put himself in the place of God, raising himself above all that is called God; in such wise that although he cannot utterly extinguish in himself all knowledge of God, he has contemned God's majesty and, as it were, made of the universe a temple wherein he himself is to be adored. "He sitteth in the temple of God, showing himself as if he were God" (II. Thess. ii., 2).[35]

This dire situation was in no small part due to the spread of Modernism, a heresy that was soundly condemned by Pius X in his landmark encyclical *Pascendi Dominici Gregis*. Before drawing the connections between Modernism and the crisis as it had developed thus far, it is important to understand what Modernism is *not*. Properly understood, it is a very specific ideology with very specific parameters (a quick perusal of *Pascendi* and its staggering level of

---

[35] Pius X, *E Supremi* (1903). https://papalencyclicals.net/pius10/p10supre.htm

Chapter 3: Naturalism

detail makes this quite clear), and Modern-*ist* is not a synonym for *modern*. The two are often conflated when they ought to be clearly distinguished.[36] Modernism is just one branch on the tree of the crisis as a whole. It was indeed a threat to the Church, and a serious one, that Pius X rightfully identified, but it could not have simply sprung out of thin air.

The central errors behind Modernism, as defined by Pius X, are *agnosticism* and *vital immanence*. Agnosticism as defined in *Pascendi* says that "human reason is confined entirely within the field of phenomena...Hence it is incapable of lifting itself up to God, and of recognizing His existence, even by means of visible things."[37] Given this belief, "what becomes of Natural Theology, of the motives of credibility, of external revelation[?] The modernists simply sweep them entirely aside; they include them in Intellectualism, which they denounce as a system

---

[36] There exists a tendency in some circles to equate these terms, unfortunately perpetuating the idea that whatever is not "traditional" and acceptable within traditionalism must be "modern" and therefore Modernist.

[37] Pius X, *Pascendi Dominici Gregis* (1907). https://papalencyclicals.net/pius10/p10pasce.htm

which is ridiculous and long since defunct."[38] Vital immanence claims religion grows from "a certain need or impulsion" and "has its origin in a movement of the heart", a movement that "must consist in a certain interior sense, originating in a need of the divine."[39] This is only possible "when natural theology has been destroyed, and the road to revelation closed by the rejection of the arguments of credibility, and all external revelation absolutely denied[.]"[40] (Pius X's successor, Pope Pius XI, put it more simply in *Mortalium Animos* when he said the Modernists "hold that dogmatic truth is not absolute but relative, that is, it agrees with the varying necessities of time and place and with the varying tendencies of the mind, since it is not contained in immutable revelation, but is capable of being accommodated to human life."[41])

Thus, it is clear that Modernism is rooted in the same errors that had been infecting the world;

---

[38] Ibid.

[39] Ibid.

[40] Ibid.

[41] Pius XI, *Mortalium Animos* (1928). https://papalencyclicals.net/pius11/p11morta.htm

namely, a denial of revelation and an exclusion of God to make way for human reason. Naturally, the Modernist's doctrines support the concept of religious indifferentism as well. As Pius X further wrote, *"Indeed Modernists do not deny but actually admit, some confusedly, others in the most open manner, that all religions are true.* That they cannot feel otherwise is clear. For on what ground, according to their theories, could falsity be predicated of any religion whatsoever?"[42]

These are compelling words from Pope Pius X, and should demonstrate beyond any doubt that this crisis of faith had already taken deep root in the world many years before Vatican II. Even before such upheavals in the 20th century as the World Wars, which accelerated the erosion of supernatural faith at an alarming pace, it was clear that bygone days were not necessarily days of spiritual triumph. As Pius X wrote in *Une Fois Encore*, "It is no longer only the Christian faith that they would uproot at all costs from the hearts of the people; it is any belief which lifting man above the horizon of this world would supernaturally bring back his wearied eyes to heaven.

---

[42] Pius X, *Pascendi Dominici Gregis*

Illusion on the subject is no longer possible. War has been declared against everything supernatural, because behind the supernatural stands God, and because it is God that they want to tear out of the mind and heart of man."[43]

The declarations of Vatican I were becoming clearer by the day as history unfolded. Naturalism had purged any influence of a higher power, and attempted to expel God and divine authority from public life and the ruling of nations. If religion is judged merely from individual standards, and civil powers attribute no more value to one religion than to another, then the very principle of authority existing outside of man-made institutions is null. Religion becomes something private and personal that individuals can choose, but it holds no authoritative precepts except those which people seemingly impose on themselves. In a summary that comprehensively concatenates the errors examined thus far, Pope Pius XI reinforced this point in his 1928 encyclical *Mortalium Animos*. Note the connection to Gregory

---

[43] Pius X, *Une Fois Encore* (1907). https://papalencyclicals.net/pius10/p10cst.htm

Chapter 3: Naturalism

XVI's *Mirari Vos*, which said that religious indifferentism is rooted in the belief that salvation can be attained through any religion as long as it upholds some form of morality.

> Since [some] hold it for certain that men destitute of all religious sense are very rarely to be found, they seem to have founded on that belief a hope that the nations, although they differ among themselves in certain religious matters, will without much difficulty come to agree as brethren in professing certain doctrines, which form as it were a common basis of the spiritual life. [...] *Certainly such attempts can nowise be approved by Catholics, founded as they are on that false opinion which considers all religions to be more or less good and praiseworthy...Not only are those who hold this opinion in error and deceived, but also in distorting the idea of true religion they reject it, and little by little, turn aside to naturalism and atheism, as it is called*; from which it clearly follows that one who supports those who hold these theories and attempt to

realize them, is altogether abandoning the divinely revealed religion.[44]

The Magisterium continued to denounce this public expulsion of morality into the 20th century, and identified it as both the root and the natural result of the two world wars. As Pope Benedict XV wrote in *Ad Beatissimi Apostolorum* in 1914:

> On every side the dread phantom of war holds sway: there is scarce room for another thought in the minds of men. [...] But it is not the present sanguinary strife alone that distresses the nations and fills Us with anxiety and care. There is another evil raging in the very inmost heart of human society, a source of dread to all who really think, inasmuch as it has already brought, and will bring, many misfortunes upon nations, and may rightly be considered to be the root cause of the present awful war. For ever since the precepts and practices of Christian wisdom ceased to be

---

[44] Pius XI, *Mortalium Animos* (1928). https://papalencyclicals.net/pius11/p11morta.htm

observed in the ruling of states, it followed that, as they contained the peace and stability of institutions, the very foundations of states necessarily began to be shaken.[45]

Following World War I, Pope Pius XI wrote in *Ubi Arcano Dei Consilio* (1922):

> There is over and above the absence of peace and the evils attendant on this absence, another deeper and more profound cause for present-day conditions. [...] Authority itself lost its hold upon mankind, for it had lost that sound and unquestionable justification for its right to command on the one hand and to be obeyed on the other. Society, quite logically and inevitably, was shaken to its very depths and even threatened with destruction, since there was left to it no longer a stable foundation, everything having been reduced to a se-

---

[45] Benedict XV, *Ad Beatissimi Apostolorum* (1914). https://papalencyclicals.net/ben15/b15adbea.htm

ries of conflicts, to the domination of the majority, or to the supremacy of special interests.

Is it to be wondered at then that, with the widespread refusal to accept the principles of true Christian wisdom, the seeds of discord sown everywhere should find a kindly soil in which to grow and should come to fruit in that most tremendous struggle, the Great War, which unfortunately did not serve to lessen but increased, by its acts of violence and of bloodshed, the international and social animosities which already existed?[46]

Pope Pius XII similarly addressed the root cause and the fallout of World War II during his pontificate. In *Summi Pontificatus* (1939), he wrote the following:[47]

---

[46] Pius XI, *Ubi Arcano Dei Consilio* (1922). https://papalencyclicals.net/pius11/p11arcan.htm

[47] Pius XII, *Summi Pontificatus* (1939). https://papalencyclicals.net/pius12/p12summi.htm

Chapter 3: Naturalism

Venerable Brethren, as We write these lines the terrible news comes to Us that the dread tempest of war is already raging despite all Our efforts to avert it. [...] The present age, Venerable Brethren, by adding new errors to the doctrinal aberrations of the past, has pushed these to extremes which lead inevitably to a drift towards chaos. *Before all else, it is certain that the radical and ultimate cause of the evils which We deplore in modern society is the denial and rejection of a universal norm of morality as well for individual and social life as for international relations*; We mean the disregard, so common nowadays, and the forgetfulness of the natural law itself, which has its foundation in God, Almighty Creator and Father of all, supreme and absolute Lawgiver, all-wise and just Judge of human actions.

For true though it is that the evils from which mankind suffers today come in part from economic instability and from the struggle of interests regarding a more equal distribution of the goods which God has

> given man as a means of sustenance and progress, *it is not less true that their root is deeper and more intrinsic, belonging to the sphere of religious belief and moral convictions which have been perverted by the progressive alienation of the peoples from that unity of doctrine, faith, customs and morals which once was promoted by the tireless and beneficent work of the Church.*

After the war, in 1947, he wrote the following in *Optatissima Pax*:[48]

> Peace, longed for so hopefully, which should signify the tranquility of order and serene liberty, even after the cruel experience of a long war, still hangs in uncertain balance, as everyone must note with sadness and alarm. Moreover, people's hearts and minds are kept in a state of anxious suspense, while in not a few nations — already laid waste by the world-conflict and its sorry aftermath of ruin

---

[48] Pius XII, *Optatissima Pax* (1947). https://papalencyclicals.net/pius12/p12optat.htm

and distress — the social classes are being incited to mutual hatred as their continuous rioting and agitation plainly threaten to subvert the very foundations of civil society.

Let all remember that the flood of evil and disaster that has over-taken the world in past years was due chiefly to the fact that the divine religion of Jesus Christ, that provider of mutual charity among citizens, peoples and nations, did not govern, as it should, private, domestic and public life.

The effects of naturalism and the abandonment of God had led to worldwide apostasy and war. Society was no longer governed by moral absolutes, leading to the pursuit of worldly things as ultimate ends instead of the things of God, and dragging many into the "abyss" (as Vatican I termed it) of materialism.

Chapter 4

Materialism

See the man who would not make God his refuge, but trusted in the abundance of his riches, and sought refuge in his wealth! (Ps 52:7)

Continuing our examination of section 7 from Vatican I's third session, the second half says the following:[49]

> The abandonment and rejection of the Christian religion, and the denial of God and his Christ, has plunged the minds of many into the abyss of pantheism, materialism and atheism, and the consequence is that they strive to destroy rational nature itself, to deny any criterion of what is right and just, and to overthrow the very foundations of human society.

---

[49] "First Vatican Council." EWTN, https://ewtn.com/catholicism/library/first-vatican-council-1505

As its name indicates, naturalism concerns itself only with the natural world, and does not permit the law of God to influence public and private life. And once this naturalism had pervaded the entire world, the Magisterium linked it to two primary consequences: an ever-increasing struggle for wealth that erupted after authority structures were removed, and the eventual pursuit of material gain as an ultimate end. When the world no longer seeks fulfillment in the divine, what is left to pursue except material things? As Pope Leo XIII wrote, "It is seen everywhere how the spirit of naturalism tends to penetrate every part of the social body, even the most healthy; a spirit which fills the minds with pride and causes them to rebel against every authority; *depraves the heart and turns it after the desire of earthly goods, neglecting those eternal.*"[50] (This passage is especially noteworthy considering it was written in the context of priestly formation. As Pope Leo further wrote, "It is greatly to be feared that some influence of this spirit, so evil, and already so widely diffused, might

---

[50] Leo XIII, *Fin Dal Principio* (1902). https://papalencyclicals.net/leo13/l13fidal.htm.

insinuate itself even among ecclesiastics, particularly among those of less experience."[51])

In examining the first facet of this materialism that had sprung from naturalism, we can look to Leo XIII's first encyclical *Inscrutabili Deo Consilio*, written in 1878:

> [F]rom the very beginning of Our pontificate, the sad sight has presented itself to Us of the evils by which the human race is oppressed on every side: the widespread subversion of the primary truths on which, as on its foundations, human society is based; the obstinacy of mind that will not brook any authority however lawful; the endless sources of disagreement, whence arrive civil strife, and ruthless war and bloodshed; the contempt of law which molds characters and is the shield of righteousness; the insatiable craving for things perishable, with complete forgetfulness of things eternal, leading up to the desperate madness whereby so many wretched

---

[51] Ibid.

beings, in all directions, scruple not to lay violent hands upon themselves[.][52]

And herein lies the first connection between the pursuit of material things and the clash between the various social classes. Again noting that the root of this evil began with spurning authority, Pope Leo warned the Church of the violence and strife that had overtaken society— a violence that would reach a climax in the Great War only a few decades later, as was further explained by Pope Benedict XV, who wrote the following in *Ad Beatissimi Apostolorum* in 1914:

> When the twofold principle of cohesion of the whole body of society has been weakened, that is to say, the union of the members with one another by mutual charity and their union with their head by their dutiful recognition of authority, is it to be wondered at, Venerable Brethren, that human society should be seen to be divided as it were into

---

[52] Leo XIII, *Inscrutabili Deo Consilio* (1878). https://papalencyclicals.net/leo13/l13evl.htm

two hostile armies bitterly and ceaselessly at strife? [...] It is not necessary to enumerate the many consequences, not less disastrous for the individual than for the community, which follow from this class hatred.

But there is still, Venerable Brethren, a deeper root of the evils we have hitherto been deploring, and unless the efforts of good men concentrate on its extirpation, that tranquil stability and peacefulness of human relations we so much desire, can never be attained. The apostle himself tells us what it is: "The desire of money is the root of all evils" (I. Tim vi. 10). If any one considers the evils under which human society is at present labouring, they will all be seen to spring from this root.

Once…there has been instilled into the minds of men that most pernicious error that man must not hope for a state of eternal happiness; but that it is here, here below, that he is to be happy in the enjoyment of wealth and honour and pleasure: what wonder that those men whose very nature was made for happiness should with all the energy which impels them to seek that very good, break down whatever delays or impedes their obtaining it. And as these goods are not equally divided amongst men, and as it is the duty of authority in the State to prevent the freedom enjoyed by the individual from going beyond its due limits and invading what belongs to another, it comes to pass that public authority is hated, and the envy of the unfortunate is inflamed against the more fortunate. Thus the struggle of one class of citizen against another bursts forth, the one trying by every means to obtain and to take what they want to have, the other endeavouring to hold and to increase what they possess.[53]

Benedict XV had described what would become the groundwork for yet a further development in this crisis; one that his successor, Pope Pius XI, would describe in the following terms in his 1937 encyclical *Divini Redemptoris*:

---

[53] Benedict XV, *Ad Beatissimi Apostolorum* (1914). https://papalencyclicals.net/ben15/b15adbea.htm

[O]ne convulsion following upon another has marked the passage of the centuries, down to the revolution of our own days. This modern revolution, it may be said, has actually broken out or threatens everywhere, and it exceeds in amplitude and violence anything yet experienced in the preceding persecutions launched against the Church. Entire peoples find themselves in danger of falling back into a barbarism worse than that which oppressed the greater part of the world at the coming of the Redeemer.

This all too imminent danger, Venerable Brethren, as you have already surmised, is bolshevistic and atheistic Communism, which aims at upsetting the social order and at undermining the very foundations of Christian civilization.[54]

And what is at the root of Communism that makes it so pernicious? As Pius XI further wrote:

---

[54] Pius XI, *Divini Redemptoris* (1937). https://papalencyclicals.net/pius11/p11divin.htm

The doctrine of modern Communism… is in substance based on the principles of dialectical and historical materialism…According to this doctrine there is in the world only one reality, matter, the blind forces of which evolve into plant, animal and man. [...] In such a doctrine, as is evident, there is no room for the idea of God; there is no difference between matter and spirit, between soul and body; there is neither survival of the soul after death nor any hope in a future life. Insisting on the dialectical aspect of their materialism, the Communists claim that the conflict which carries the world towards its final synthesis can be accelerated by man. Hence they endeavor to sharpen the antagonisms which arise between the various classes of society. Thus the class struggle with its consequent violent hate and destruction takes on the aspects of a crusade for the progress of humanity.[55]

---

[55] Ibid.

Tracing it back even further and finding this materialism rooted in naturalism, Pius XI also wrote, "When religion is banished from the school, from education and from public life, when the representatives of Christianity and its sacred rites are held up to ridicule, are we not really fostering the materialism which is the fertile soil of Communism?"[56] The words of Vatican I were indeed accurate, as were the warnings of the popes before this time. The pattern of forces working against the Church had continued to follow a tragically predictable path. The social order was governed by nothing except the pursuit of wealth and prosperity, and torn apart by the subsequent struggle for power.

A second aspect of this materialism is the pursuit of pleasure amidst a society shaken by war and attempting to recover. Just as he denounced the materialism at the root of Communism, Pope Pius XI seized the opportunity to identify the growing inclination toward material frivolity that was sprouting in the 20th century. None would debate the sudden increase in technological advancements during this

---

[56] Ibid.

time, whether for weapons in the Great War, communication, entertainment, or otherwise. The trends toward leisure, entertainment, and indulgence were becoming more prominent, undoubtedly as an escape from the horrors of war and the gloom it had brought over civilization, but an escape that may unfortunately have given way to excessive pursuit of distractions and enjoyments. And, in a world that has been influenced by the casting off of religious guidelines and sound morality, the means by which the people sought to be entertained were not influenced by a Christian spirit.

In 1929, Pius XI wrote the following in *Divini Illius Magistri*:

> More than ever nowadays an extended and careful vigilance is necessary, inasmuch as the dangers of moral and religious shipwreck are greater for inexperienced youth. Especially is this true of impious and immoral books, often diabolically circulated at low prices; of the cinema, which multiplies every kind of exhibition; and now also of the radio,

which facilitates every kind of communications. These most powerful means of publicity, which can be of great utility for instruction and education when directed by sound principles, are only too often used as an incentive to evil passions and greed for gain. [...] How often today must parents and educators bewail the corruption of youth brought about by the modern theater and the vile book![57]

His warnings about the cinema and its influence were further drawn out in his encyclical *Vigilanti Cura* in 1936:

> Now then, it is a certainty which can readily be verified that the more marvellous the progress of the motion picture art and industry, the more pernicious and deadly has it shown itself to morality and to religion and even to the very decencies of human society.

---

[57] Pius XI, *Divini Illius Magistri* (1929). https://papalencyclicals.net/pius11/p11rappr.htm

[A]t the very age when the moral sense is being formed and when the notions and sentiments of justice and rectitude, of duty and obligation and of ideals of life are being developed, the motion picture with its direct propaganda assumes a position of commanding influence.

So much so that when one thinks of the havoc wrought in the souls of youth and of childhood, of the loss of innocence so often suffered in the motion picture theatres, there comes to mind the terrible condemnation pronounced by Our Lord upon the corrupters of little ones: *"whosoever shall scandalize one of these little ones who believe in Me, it were better for him that a millstone be hanged about his neck and that he be drowned in the depths of the sea"*.

Indeed the effectiveness of our schools, of our Catholic associations, and even of our churches is lessened and endangered by the plague of evil and pernicious motion pictures.[58]

How much more do these words apply today, when the entertainment industry has dominated so much of our time, and when we often give more thought to how we can spend our free time in distracting ourselves than with deepening our spiritual lives? How much more explicit and immoral have many of our movies, shows, and other forms of entertainment become since Pius XI warned us of this almost one hundred years ago?

This would later be echoed by Pius XII in his encyclical *Miranda Prorsus* in 1957:

> During the past century the technological progress made by industry has often had this result, that the machines which were intended to serve man have actually reduced him to serfdom, to his great loss. And so today the mounting technological advances in

---

[58] Pius XI, *Vigilanti Cura* (1936). https://papalencyclicals.net/pius11/p11vigil.htm (emphasis in original)

communicating pictures, sounds, and ideas must be subjected to the sweet yoke of the law of Christ if they are not to become a source of countless evils which will be all the more serious in that they will enslave not only the powers of nature but also those of the soul.

…We cannot approve the stand of those who claim and defend their freedom to depict and display whatever they please, despite the perfectly evident fact that great harm has come to souls in days past as a result of this attitude. For here the issue is not real freedom, which We have discussed above, but unchecked license to express oneself without regard for prudence, even though this be contrary to sound morals and liable to result in serious danger for souls.[59]

That same year, Pius XII wrote the following in *La Perelinage de Lourdes*:

---

[59] Pius XII, *Miranda Prorsus* (1957). https://papalencyclicals.net/pius12/p12miran.htm

Chapter 4: Materialism

But the world, which today affords so many justifiable reasons for pride and hope, is also undergoing a terrible temptation to materialism which has been denounced by Our Predecessors and Ourselves on many occasions.

This materialism is not confined to that condemned philosophy which dictates the policies and economy of a large segment of mankind. It rages also in a love of money which creates ever greater havoc as modern enterprises expand, and which, unfortunately, determines many of the decisions which weigh heavy on the life of the people. It finds expression in the cult of the body, in excessive desire for comforts, and in flight from all the austerities of life. It encourages scorn for human life, even for life which is destroyed before seeing the light of day.

This materialism is present in the unrestrained search for pleasure, which flaunts itself shamelessly and tries, through reading matter and entertainments, to seduce souls which are still pure. It shows itself in lack of interest in one's brother, in selfishness which crushes him, in justice which deprives him of his rights — in a word, in that concept of life which regulates everything exclusively in terms of material prosperity and earthly satisfactions.[60]

It should be readily clear that seeking ultimate fulfillment in material things leads to the weakening of pursuit toward spiritual things, bringing apathy and a faith that is lived externally but without conviction. As Pius XII wrote elsewhere, "What age has been, for all its technical and purely civic progress, more tormented than ours by spiritual emptiness and deep-felt interior poverty?"[61] And it is this which would become the next and final element of this crisis of faith.

---

[60] Pius XII, *La Perelinage de Lourdes* (1957). https://papalencyclicals.net/pius12/p12peler.htm

[61] Pius XII, *Summi Pontificatus* (1939). https://papalencyclicals.net/pius12/p12summi.htm

Chapter 5

Catholics in Name Only

But they flattered him with their mouths; they lied to him with their tongues. Their heart was not steadfast toward him; they were not true to his covenant. (Ps 78:36-37)

The eighth section of Vatican I's third session, and the last in our examination of the crisis, reads as follows:

> 8. With this impiety spreading in every direction, it has come about, alas, that many even among the children of the Catholic Church have strayed from the path of genuine piety, and as the truth was gradually diluted in them, their Catholic sensibility was weakened. Led away by diverse and strange teachings and confusing nature and grace, human knowledge and divine faith, they are found to distort the genuine sense of the dogmas which Holy mother Church holds and

teaches, and to endanger the integrity and genuineness of the faith.[62]

The world's slow drip of water on the rock of truth during the preceding decades had worn away the influence of the Catholic faith on the moral life of civilization, and the faith was becoming more of an external facade than a rightly ordered interior disposition.

In our present time, it is common to hear people referred to as "Catholics in name only", and unfortunately there is good reason for this. There are many who call themselves Catholic but who do not act as such. They attend Mass on major feast days and for personal circumstances like weddings or funerals, but hardly ever otherwise; they know little about the tenets of their faith; they publicly voice support for ideas and propositions that have been soundly condemned by the Church. They do not conduct themselves as a Catholic should, yet despite all these things, they insist on calling themselves Catholic, ultimately treating it as little more than a social marker.

---

[62] "First Vatican Council." EWTN, https://ewtn.com/catholicism/library/first-vatican-council-1505

Chapter 5: Catholics in Name Only

This is yet again an example of a very real issue that is often blamed on the reforms of the Second Vatican Council, but this is by no means a problem that is unique to the present time. Certainly, if it was an error that the Church had deplored almost a century prior, it was already widespread.

Briefly returning to the period before the turn of the 20th century, we find that Pope Leo XIII had already identified this concern on a number of occasions, some implicit and some quite explicit. The first of several notable instances was in his 1890 encyclical *Sapientiae Christianae*. His predecessors, as we have seen, had been ringing the alarm bells for some time on the progressively weakening influence of Christianity, and before any direct mention of this issue, Leo XIII made it clear that apathy had crept into the Christian way of life.

> Whence it appears how urgent is the duty to maintain perfect union of minds, especially at these our times, when the Christian name is assailed with designs so concerted and subtle. [...] This is not now the time and

place to inquire whether and how far the inertness and internal dissensions of Catholics have contributed to the present condition of things; but it is certain at least that the perverse-minded would exhibit less boldness, and would not have brought about such an accumulation of ills, if the faith "which worketh by charity" had been generally more energetic and lively in the souls of men, and had there not been so universal a drifting away from the divinely established rule of morality throughout Christianity.[63]

To think that the inspiration of a once deeply-held faith was beginning to lose its hold even before the world wars and Communism is indeed cause for concern.

The very next year, in his 1891 encyclical on the Rosary, *Octobri Mense*, Leo XIII made explicit reference to those who profess to be Catholic but do not show it in practice. In calling attention to "universal and well-known" evils which afflicted the Church,

---

[63] Leo XIII, *Sapientiae Christianae* (1890). https://papalencyclicals.net/leo13/l13sapie.htm

including "war made upon the sacred dogmas which the Church holds...derision cast upon the integrity of that Christian morality which she has in keeping; enmity declared, with the impudence of audacity and with criminal malice, against the very Christ"[64] he acknowledged that these evils are not a new threat, but that they had affected Catholics to such a degree that the following warning was necessary (and notably, that this was an error that had developed in tandem with religious indifferentism): "It is indeed a cause of great sorrow that so many should be deterred and led astray by error and enmity to God; that so many should be indifferent to all forms of religion, and should finally become estranged from faith; *that so many Catholics should be such in name only, and should pay to religion no honor or worship.*"[65]

This is quite a striking warning. *So many* Catholics! *So many* others indifferent to any forms of religion or supernatural faith! We see yet another connection between this tragedy of externalized piety and religious indifferentism when Pope Leo XIII

---

[64] Leo XIII, *Octobri Mense* (1891). https://papalencyclicals.net/leo13/l13ro1.htm

[65] Ibid.

again referred to it in his 1892 encyclical *Inimica Vis*, on Freemasonry. As we have already demonstrated, a core tenet of Freemasonry is religious indifferentism, and in lamenting this sect's influence, Leo XIII wrote, "It is commonly claimed that the ancient ardor of spirit in protecting their ancestral faith has grown cold among the Italian people. *Nor is this perhaps false; especially since if the dispositions of both sides be inspected, those who wage war on religion seem to show more energy than those who repel it.*"[66]

Directly connecting this lack of conviction to the aforementioned materialism, Pope St. Pius X wrote in his encyclical *Acerbo Nimis*:

> It is a common complaint, unfortunately too well founded, that there are large numbers of Christians in our own time who are entirely ignorant of those truths necessary for salvation. And when we mention Christians, We refer not only to the masses or to those in the lower walks of life…but We refer to those especially who do not lack culture or talents

---

[66] Leo XIII, *Inimica Vis* (1892). https://papalencyclicals.net/leo13/l13ms4.htm

and, indeed, are possessed of abundant knowledge regarding things of the world but live rashly and imprudently with regard to religion.

There is then, Venerable Brethren, no reason for wonder that the corruption of morals and depravity of life is already so great, and ever increasingly greater, not only among uncivilized peoples but even in those very nations that are called Christian.[67]

If we wish to focus our examination to something concrete, a more particular example can be found in connection with employment and public life. As Pope Pius XI wrote in *Divini Redemptoris* in 1937:

The minds of men must be illuminated with the sure light of Catholic teaching, and their wills must be drawn to follow and apply it as the norm of right living in the conscientious fulfillment of their manifold social duties. Thus they will oppose that incoherence

---

[67] Pius X, *Acerbo Nimis (1905)*. https://papalencyclicals.net/pius10/p10chdoc.htm

and discontinuity in Christian life which We have many times lamented. *For there are some who, while exteriorly faithful to the practice of their religion, yet in the field of labor and industry, in the professions, trade and business, permit a deplorable cleavage in their conscience, and live a life too little in conformity with the clear principles of justice and Christian charity.* Such lives are a scandal to the weak, and to the malicious a pretext to discredit the Church.[68]

As an example of this disparity between Catholic belief and conduct in one's employment, we might again look to Pius XI's encyclical *Vigilanti Cura*, in which he said of the motion picture industry, "There are surely many Catholics among the executives, directors, authors, and actors who take part in this business, *and it is unfortunate that their influence has not always been in accordance with their Faith and with their ideals.* You will do well, Venerable Brethren, to pledge them to bring their profession into

---

[68] Pius XI, *Divini Redemptoris* (1937). https://papalencyclicals.net/pius11/p11divin.htm

harmony with their conscience as respectable men and followers of Jesus Christ."[69] This is all the more concerning when he said of this industry that "there does not exist today a means of influencing the masses more potent than the cinema" and "[i]t is unfortunate that, in the present state of affairs, this influence is frequently exerted for evil"[70]—a statement which is all the more relevant to our present time.

But perhaps the most explicit papal warning was the following passage from *Divini Redemptoris* in 1937:

> *Even in Catholic countries there are still too many who are Catholics hardly more than in name.* There are too many who fulfill more or less faithfully the more essential obligations of the religion they boast of professing, but have no desire of knowing it better, of deepening their inward conviction, and still less of bringing into conformity with the external gloss the inner splendor of a right and

---

[69] Pius XI, *Vigilanti Cura* (1936). https://papalencyclicals.net/pius11/p11vigil.htm

[70] Ibid.

unsullied conscience, that recognizes and performs all its duties under the eye of God. We know how much Our Divine Savior detested this empty pharisaic show, He Who wished that all should adore the Father "in spirit and in truth." The Catholic who does not live really and sincerely according to the Faith he professes will not long be master of himself in these days when the winds of strife and persecution blow so fiercely, but will be swept away defenseless in this new deluge which threatens the world. And thus, while he is preparing his own ruin, he is exposing to ridicule the very name of Christian.[71]

These repeated warnings should give us pause (especially considering Pius XI wrote the previous passage in connection to the spread of Communism, saying, "It can surprise no one that the Communistic fallacy should be spreading in a world already to a large extent de-Christianized").[72] For centuries, the

---

[71] Pius XI, *Divini Redemptoris* (1937). https://papalencyclicals.net/pius11/p11divin.htm

[72] Ibid.

Chapter 5: Catholics in Name Only

attractiveness of modernity had been overpowering the influence of spiritual realities that had long been a primary and powerful safeguard. Great advancements in technology, the Industrial Revolution, and other historical events were beginning to make humanity believe it could be self-sufficient, and religion characterized so strongly by obedience to authority was losing its hold as humanity rejected any spiritual authorities over itself. As Pope Pius XI wrote in *Ingravescentibus Malis* that same year, "[B]ecause the supreme and eternal authority of God, which commands and forbids, is despised and completely repudiated by men, *the result is that the consciousness of Christian duty is weakened, and that faith becomes tepid in souls or entirely lost*, and his afterward affects and ruins the very basis of human society."[73]

And what effect might this have beyond the circles of the laity? It is from this flock that the young men entering seminary come, a flock which has tragically been hampered by inertness and lack of zeal for their faith. This is yet another commonly cited argu-

---

[73] Pius XI, *Ingravescentibus Malis* (1937). https://papalencyclicals.net/pius11/p11grave.htm

ment by those who see the reforms of the 20th century as the root cause of the crisis; that the plummeting numbers of vocations are due to a "new" understanding of the ministerial priesthood. But perhaps the answer is much simpler. Pope Pius XI wrote in *Ad Catholici Sacerdotii* in 1935:

> The lack of vocations in families of the middle and upper classes may be partly explained by the dissipations of modern life, the seductions, which especially in the larger cities, prematurely awaken the passions of youth; the schools in many places which scarcely conduce to the development of vocations. *Nevertheless, it must be admitted that such a scarcity reveals a deplorable falling off of faith in the families themselves.* Did they indeed look at things in the light of faith, what greater dignity could Christian parents desire for their sons, what ministry more noble, than that which, as We have said, is worthy of the veneration of men and angels?[74]

---

[74] Pius XI, *Ad Catholici Sacerdotii* (1935). https://papalencyclicals.net/pius11/p11catho.htm

Note that Pius XI describes this concern in tandem with "middle and upper class" families. We should again recall the papal warnings of the last chapter and how the pull of materialism had been overpowering the adherence to religion for some time, and where there was wealth and opulence, there was a dwindling interest in the things of the Church. (Another similar passage from this encyclical is worthy of note: "Whoever, on the other hand, urged on, perhaps, by ill-advised parents, looks to this state as a means to temporal and earthly gains which he imagines and desires in the priesthood, *as happened more often in the past*...show that they are not intended for the priesthood."[75]) The answer to the question of the vocations crisis may be much simpler than theological subtleties. It may simply be that a weak faith was motivating fewer men to enter the seminary, and perhaps those who did were not driven by a strong faith in the first place.

As our final example, we can look to the writings of Pope Pius XII. Of the years preceding his pontificate, he wrote in his first encyclical *Summi Pontificatus*:

---

[75] Ibid.

What heart is not inflamed, is not swept forward to help at the sight of so many brothers and sisters who, misled by error, passion, temptation and prejudice, have strayed away from faith in the true God and have lost contact with the joyful and life-giving message of Christ? [...] Who could observe without profound grief the tragic harvest of such desertions among those who in days of calm and security were numbered among the followers of Christ, but who — *Christians unfortunately more in name than in fact* — in the hour that called for endurance, for effort, for suffering, for a stout heart in face of hidden or open persecution, fell victims of cowardice, weakness, uncertainty; who, terror-stricken before the sacrifices entailed by a profession of their Christian Faith, could not steel themselves to drink the bitter chalice awaiting those faithful to Christ?[76]

---

[76] Pius XII, *Summi Pontificatus* (1939). https://papalencyclicals.net/pius12/p12summi.htm

Then, addressing the second World Congress for the Lay Apostolate in 1957 (a congress whose theme was appropriately titled "Laymen in the Crisis of the Modern World: Responsibilities and Training"), he wrote that the coming years demanded a formation characterized by "[g]reater knowledge of the faith", saying: "*In this respect, laymen are too often illiterate. There is danger of a lack of balance between a temporal culture which is ever more highly developed and a religious culture which would remain childish. If he is to share his faith with others, the apostle must find his strength in the word of God and in the liturgy. He must live in 'the charity of faith.'*"[77]

These papal warnings may give us reason to reconsider any notions we might have about the mid-20th century being a pinnacle of Catholic history. This is not to issue a sweeping judgment that anything and everything was a facade. We of course cannot generalize in such broad terms. However, the fact that several pontiffs issued direct and explicit warnings about external displays of piety masking interior apathy should be sobering for us. But neither should

---

[77] Pius XII, *Guiding Principles for the Lay Apostolate* (1957). https://papalencyclicals.net/pius12/ p12layap.htm

it come as a surprise. If the previously mentioned errors had been entangling their roots in society for centuries prior, it may very well have become easy to maintain an appearance of Catholicity, perhaps associating it with one's cultural or familial heritage to a greater degree than being interiorly convicted by its core beliefs. And, as we shall see, a pious gloss could only sustain itself for so long once confronted with the dawning of the technological age.

Chapter 6

A New Era

The fool says in his heart, "There is no God." They are corrupt, they do abominable deeds, there is none that does good. (Ps 14:1)

Where do we find ourselves in the mid-20th century?

Recovering from two global wars that had decimated entire cities and populations, the world was at the beginning of a new era, an era of scientific conquest, increased means of production, and new forms of entertainment. There was increased mingling of cultures and customs through global connection and travel. Television, radio, and the cinema were already widespread, bringing new ideas and new modes of transmitting entertainment not only into every town, but into every home (and unbeknownst to the world at the time, the digital age was not far in the future). Technology that was once only available to social elites was now available to all. And in a post-war environment, the world was eager to rebound away from the death and destruction it had faced, taking comfort in its new inventions, methods, and ideas to pursue a better future.

Some see this time period as a kind of "golden age" of Catholicism. But it may surprise us to learn that many of the issues that are lamented today were already present during this time. Pope Pius XII deplored the fact that during his pontificate, "devotion to the Virgin Mother of God…is so neglected, especially among the young, as to fade away and gradually vanish;"[78] that there were "clergy who make light of or lessen esteem for frequent confession;"[79] and that some "do not think it suitable to re-enkindle the spirit of piety in modern times"[80] with regard to devotions.[81] Even the complaint so common today

---

[78] Pius XII, *Mediator Dei* (1947). https://papalencyclicals.net/pius12/p12media.htm

[79] Pius XII, *Mystici Corporis* (1943). https://papalencyclicals.net/pius12/p12mysti.htm

[80] Pius XII, *Haurietis Aquas* (1956). https://papalencyclicals.net/pius12/p12hauri.htm

[81] Some other noteworthy examples include Pope Benedict XV's admonishment to the laity about their immodest attire at Mass in *Sacra Propediem* (1921), or Pius XI's rebuke about neglecting observation of the Lord's

about the conduct of certain priests was one that Pius XII identified in his 1950 encyclical *Menti Nostrae:*

> The age in which we live suffers from serious errors indeed: philosophical systems which are born and die without improving morals in any way; monstrosities of art which even pretend to call themselves Christian; standards of government in many countries which are aimed at the personal interests of individuals rather than at the common prosperity of all; methods of living and economic and social relations which threaten honest men more than the cunning. From this it follows almost naturally that there are not lacking in our times priests, infected in some way by this contagion, who imbibe opinions and follow a mode of life even in dress and the care of their person alien to both their dignity and their mission; priests who allow themselves to be led astray by the mania for novelty whether it be in their preaching to the

---

Day for the sake of sporting activities in *Mit Brennender Sorge* (1937).

faithful or in combating the errors of adversaries; priests who compromise not only their consciences but also their good name and the efficacy of their ministry.[82]

We would do well to heed the continued warnings of Pope Pius XII, who wrote the following in *Anni Sacri* in 1950:

> On the part of not a few religion is passed by as a thing of no importance, and elsewhere absolutely prohibited in family and social life as a remnant of ancient superstitions; public and private atheism is exalted in such a way that God and His law are being abolished, and morals no longer have any foundation.[83]

There can be no doubt that by this point in time, a crisis of faith was festering in the world, reaching

---

[82] Pius XII, *Menti Nostrae* (1950). https://papalencyclicals.net/pius12/p12clerg.htm

[83] Pius XII, *Anni Sacri* (1950). https://papalencyclicals.net/pius12/p12anni.htm

its tendrils into the home, the schools, the government, and even the seminaries. A radical individualism had slowly and patiently eaten away at the foundations of charity and love that once served as the guiding forces of civilization. Where once was promoted service and selflessness towards our neighbors, now only opportunities for advancement and domination were seen. When piety, contemplation, and prayer once occupied spare time, now there was the instant gratification of mass media to fill that inner desire. The very idea of God, which was once a uniting bond between families and communities, was simply forgotten. The situation was indeed bleak and could not continue this way for much longer without undergoing complete collapse.

In 1958, Pope John XXIII was elected to the papacy. Several of his encyclicals directly address the sources of the crisis in the context of his time at the dawn of a new scientifically-driven era, and must be examined before proceeding.

Echoing the words of Pius XII about the disconnect between scientific advancement and religious formation, he wrote in *Pacem in Terris* (1963):

It is...clear that today, in traditionally Christian nations, secular institutions, although demonstrating a high degree of scientific and technical perfection...not infrequently are but slightly affected by Christian motivation or inspiration.

It is beyond question that in the creation of those institutions many contributed and continue to contribute who were believed to be and who consider themselves Christians; and without doubt, in part at least, they were and are. How does one explain this? *It is Our opinion that the explanation is to be found in an inconsistency in their minds between religious belief and their action in the temporal sphere.*

It is Our opinion, too, that the above-mentioned inconsistency between the religious faith in those who believe and their activities in the temporal sphere, results — in great part — from the lack of a solid Christian education. Indeed, it happens in many quarters and too often that there is no proportion between scientific training and religious instruction: the former continues and is extended until it reaches higher degrees, while the latter remains at elementary level.[84]

This unfortunate tendency to prioritize scientific knowledge over spiritual growth is directly connected to the trend towards materialism, of which he wrote in *Ad Petri Cathedram* (1959):

> So much toil and effort is expended today in mastering and advancing human knowledge that our age glories — and rightly — in the amazing progress it has made in the field of scientific research. *But why do we not devote as much energy, ingenuity, and enthusiasm to the sure and safe attainment of that learning which concerns not this earthly, mortal life but the life which lies ahead of us in heaven?* Our spirit will rest in peace and joy only when we have reached that truth which

---

[84] John XXIII, *Pacem in Terris* (1963). https://papalencyclicals.net/john23/j23pacem.htm

is taught in the gospels and which should be reduced to action in our lives.[85]

His allusions to the errors of naturalism are clear. On naturalism itself, he wrote the following in *Mater et Magistra* (1961):

> *The most perniciously typical aspect of the modern era consists in the absurd attempt to reconstruct a solid and fruitful temporal order divorced from God, who is, in fact, the only foundation on which it can endure.* In seeking to enhance man's greatness, men fondly imagine that they can do so by drying up the source from which that greatness springs and from which it is nourished. They want, that is, to restrain and, if possible, to eliminate the soul's upward surge toward God. But today's experience of so much disillusionment and bloodshed only goes to confirm those words

---

[85] John XXIII, *Ad Petri Cathedram* (1959). https://papalencyclicals.net/john23/j23petri.htm

of Scripture: "Unless the Lord build the house, they labor in vain that build it."[86]

And without the Lord as the source of their action, the work of men is not directed toward the pursuit of truth. Of indifferentism, Pope John wrote the following in *Ad Petri Cathedram*:

> Some men, indeed...act as though God had given us intellects for some purpose other than the pursuit and attainment of truth. *This mistaken sort of action leads directly to that absurd proposition: one religion is just as good as another, for there is no distinction here between truth and falsehood.* [...] [T]o contend that there is nothing to choose between contradictories and among contraries can lead only to this fatal conclusion: a reluctance to accept any religion either in theory or practice.
>
> *How can God, who is truth, approve or tolerate the indifference, neglect, and sloth of*

---

[86] John XXIII, *Mater et Magistra* (1961). https://papalencyclicals.net/john23/j23mater.htm

those who attach no importance to matters on which our eternal salvation depends; who attach no importance to pursuit and attainment of necessary truths, or to the offering of that proper worship which is owed to God alone?[87]

And finally, in this same encyclical, Pope John XXIII directly addressed the ultimate root of this crisis, a root that links all the previously described errors together throughout the centuries:

All the evils which poison men and nations and trouble so many hearts have a single cause and a single source: ignorance of the truth — and at times even more than ignorance, a contempt for truth and a reckless rejection of it. Thus arise all manner of errors, which enter the recesses of men's hearts and the bloodstream of human society as would a plague.[88]

---

[87] John XXIII, *Ad Petri Cathedram* (1959). https://papalencyclicals.net/john23/j23petri.htm

[88] Ibid.

Chapter 6: A New Era

The world had reached a turning point, and John XXIII knew it. In a decision that was as unexpected as it was historic, Pope John announced his plans for a new council in 1959. He was seen by many as a pope who would simply maintain the status quo and not make any significant decisions during his pontificate, but just several months after his election, those expectations were shattered.

Many people, even today, ask: why was Vatican II actually called?

Councils can be called for any number of reasons: to condemn specific heresies (such as the Council of Nicaea), to restore ecclesiastical discipline (as in the case of Lateran I), or to define new dogma (as with Vatican I). These objectives often overlap, but ultimately, councils are gathered so that the Church can address the pressing needs of the time, whatever those needs may be. In the case of Vatican II, Pope John XXIII very directly explained the need for a council. In his Apostolic Constitution *Humanae Salutis*, he wrote:

> *Today the Church is witnessing a crisis underway within society.* While humanity is at

the threshold of a new age, immensely serious and broad tasks await the Church, as in the most tragic periods of her history. It is a question in fact of bringing the perennial life-giving energies of the Gospel to the modern world, a world that boasts of its technical and scientific conquests but also bears the effects of a temporal order that some have wanted to reorganize by excluding God. This is why modern society is characterized by great material progress but without a corresponding advance in the moral sphere. Thence a weakening in aspirations towards the values of the spirit; thence the tendency to seek only the earthly pleasures that technological progress brings so easily within the reach of all; thence also a quite new and disturbing fact: the existence of a militant atheism operating all over the world.[89]

---

[89] "Pope John XXIII Convokes the Second Vatican Council," trans. Joseph A. Komonchak, https://jakomonchak.wordpress.com/wp-content/uploads/2011/12/humanae-salutis.pdf

What better way for the Church to respond to this worldwide "militant" crisis than to assemble in a general council and carve out a pathway forward to restore the spiritual foundations that once had supported all of mankind? Pope John XXIII felt there was a need to rejuvenate the Church's missionary activity and bring Christ out to the world, "in order to give the Church the possibility to contribute more effectively to the solutions of the problems of the modern age."[90] The objective was not "to discuss certain fundamentals of Catholic doctrine, or to restate in greater detail the traditional teaching of the Fathers and of early and more recent theologians. There was no need to call a council merely to hold discussions of that nature."[91] What was needed was "a new enthusiasm, a new joy and serenity of mind in the unreserved acceptance by all of the entire Christian faith, without forfeiting that accuracy and precision in its presentation which characterized the proceedings of the Council of Trent and the First Vatican

---

[90] Ibid.

[91] Pope Saint John XXIII, "Opening Address To the Council," Catholic Culture, https://www.catholicculture.org/culture/library/view.cfm?recnum=3233

Council."[92] Pope John XXIII's wish was that Catholic doctrine should be "more widely known, more deeply understood, and more penetrating in its effects on men's moral lives."[93]

The objectives of the Council were further explained in the introduction to the first document that was discussed— *Sacrosanctum Concilium*, the decree on the sacred liturgy. As was declared in this document, the Council's intention was fourfold; to "impart an ever increasing vigor to the Christian life of the faithful; to adapt more suitably to the needs of our own times those institutions which are subject to change; to foster whatever can promote union among all who believe in Christ; to strengthen whatever can help to call the whole of mankind into the household of the Church."[94]

The Church had read the signs of the times and realized that a necessary restoration of the Christian

---

[92] Ibid.

[93] Ibid.

[94] Paul VI, Constitution on the Sacred Liturgy *Sacrosanctum Concilium* (1963). Vatican Archive, https://vatican.va/archive/hist_councils/ii_vatican_council/documents/vat-ii_const_19631204_sacrosanctum-concilium_en.html

way of life was most opportune at this time, both because of the fading of Christian influence on public life, but also because of the developments in the world which were providing opportunities for the Gospel to be spread. Methods of instant and far-reaching communication were more prevalent. Nations and communities were increasingly blending with others, mixing cultures and ideas in a way the world had not yet experienced. Perhaps most importantly, the Church knew that the world which for so long had turned its back on Christ would soon realize its erroneous ways and return to the truth like the prodigal son, once worldly pursuits showed themselves to be unfulfilling. It was "necessary for [the Church] to keep up to date with the changing conditions of this modern world, and of modern living, for these have opened up entirely new avenues for the Catholic apostolate."[95] The Council's maxim might well be summed up in the words of Pope Benedict XV from 1914: "Old things, but in a new way."[96]

---

[95] Pope Saint John XXIII, "Opening Address To the Council".

[96] Benedict XV, *Ad Beatissimi Apostolorum* (1914). https://papalencyclicals.net/ben15/b15adbea.htm

Vatican II was very different from other councils in the way it presented its teachings. Previously, the Church had pronounced a teaching or a belief, with an anathema on the opposite. But Vatican II took a different approach. It is important to remember that it was trying to build up the spiritual lives of people and communities, and its various documents reflect this in their collective effort to plant new seeds for the growth of a renewed Christian spirit. The Council's four constitutions speak directly to the root causes of the crisis explored thus far:

❖ The Dogmatic Constitution on Divine Revelation, *Dei Verbum*, intended to "set forth authentic doctrine on divine revelation and how it is handed on, so that by hearing the message of salvation the whole world may believe, by believing it may hope, and by hoping it may love."[97]

---

[97] Paul VI, Dogmatic Constitution on Divine Revelation *Dei Verbum* (1965). Vatican Archive, https://vatican.va/archive/hist_councils/ii_vatican_council/documents/vat-ii_const_19651118_dei-verbum_en.html

- ❖ The Dogmatic Constitution on the Church, *Lumen Gentium*, explained that the Church desired to "unfold more fully to the faithful of the Church and to the whole world its own inner nature and universal mission. [...] The present-day conditions of the world add greater urgency to this work of the Church so that all men, joined more closely today by various social, technical and cultural ties, might also attain fuller unity in Christ."[98]
- ❖ The Pastoral Constitution on the Church in the Modern World, *Gaudium et Spes*, voiced the Council's wish to "explain to everyone how it conceives of the presence and activity of the Church in the world of today" and to "speak to all men in order to shed light on the mystery of man and to cooperate in finding the solution to the outstanding problems of our time."[99]

---

[98] Paul VI, Dogmatic Constitution on the Church *Lumen Gentium* (1964). Vatican Archive, https://www.vatican.va/archive/hist_councils/ii_vatican_council/documents/vat-ii_const_19641121_lumen-gentium_en.html

[99] Paul VI, Pastoral Constitution on the Church in the Modern World *Gaudium et Spes* (1965). Vatican Archive,

❖ The Constitution on the Sacred Liturgy, *Sacrosanctum Concilium*, called for a reform of the sacred liturgy so that "the sanctification of men in Christ and the glorification of God, to which all other activities of the Church are directed as toward their end, is achieved in the most efficacious possible way."[100]

Its other various decrees and declarations similarly spoke to the Church's mission of evangelization, providing long, theological meditations as material for discussion, prayer, and study. They urge people to explore the spiritual treasuries of the Church, especially the Scriptures, and are meant to act as a leaven to a faith that had grown weak, giving opportunities for new growth instead of pruning and trimming as previous councils had done. Instead of declaring what Catholics may *not* do or believe, they state what Catholics *should* do and believe. Instead of

---

https://www.vatican.va/archive/hist_councils/ii_vatican_council/documents/vat-ii_cons_19651207_gaudium-et-spes_en.html

[100] Paul VI, Constitution on the Sacred Liturgy *Sacrosanctum Concilium*.

shining a spotlight on one particular error or heresy, as many previous councils had, they explain the ideological errors behind the troubles the world faces and how the Church can provide fulfillment in place of them.[101] The Council's primary objective was not to denounce error, but to laud truth.

The ambitions of the Council were lofty, and would take time to be fully realized. It is certainly true that in the years after, there was confusion about what the Council intended, what its teachings actually consisted of, and how they might best be implemented. Seeds were planted, but the field in which they were planted had long been overgrown with weeds, and it may have been that the first step in this renewal was to expose the stagnation and the decay lurking underneath the external facade of a thriving Church. But to some, it appeared that this attempt at renewal had brought the decay, rather than simply

---

[101] A common criticism of Vatican II is that it did not directly condemn Communism, but this misses the fact that atheistic Communism and its detrimental effects on the world is precisely the reason the council was called in the first place!

exposing it. This brings us to the original question: when and how did this crisis really begin?

Chapter 7

The True Source of the Crisis

[T]hey were rebellious in their purposes, and were brought low through their iniquity. (Ps 106:43)

Let us return to the passages from Session 3 of Vatican I. What was it that gave way to private judgment, religious indifferentism, naturalism, materialism, and apathy? What caused the Council to make known the Church's concern over the errors that were developing? From what root cause comes this deadly ignorance that has generated so many other wounds in the world and the Church?

For a summary of the entire time period examined thus far, we can look to Pope Pius XII, who wrote the following in *Summi Pontificatus* in 1939:

> The denial of the fundamentals of morality had its origin, in Europe, in the abandonment of that Christian teaching of which the Chair of Peter is the depository and exponent. That teaching had once given spiritual

cohesion to a Europe which, educated, ennobled and civilized by the Cross, had reached such a degree of civil progress as to become the teacher of other peoples, of other continents. But, cut off from the infallible teaching authority of the Church, not a few separated brethren have gone so far as to overthrow the central dogma of Christianity, the Divinity of the Savior, and have hastened thereby the progress of spiritual decay.[102]

There is an unmistakable thread running throughout the many magisterial sources cited thus far. Their explanations of the crisis and how it grew are sufficient to make very clear what the true source of the crisis is. But to ensure there is no question about this, the following quotes make the Magisterium's universal assessment known:

- ❖ Pope Leo XII in 1824: "[I]f one wishes to search out the true source of all the evils which We have already lamented, as well as those which

---

[102] Pius XII, *Summi Pontificatus* (1939). https://papalencyclicals.net/pius12/p12summi.htm

We pass over for the sake of brevity, he will surely find that from the start it has ever been a dogged contempt for the Church's authority."[103]

❖ Pope Leo XIII in 1878: "Now, the source of these evils lies chiefly, We are convinced, in this, that the holy and venerable authority of the Church, which in God's name rules mankind, upholding and defending all lawful authority, has been despised and set aside."[104]

❖ Pope Benedict XV in 1914: "The…cause of the general unrest we declare to be the absence of respect for the authority of those who exercise ruling powers. Ever since the source of human powers has been sought apart from God the Creator and Ruler of the Universe, in the free will of men, the bonds of duty, which should exist between superior and inferior, have been so weakened as almost to have ceased to exist.

---

[103] Leo XII, *Ubi Primum* (1824). https://papalencyclicals.net/leo12/l12ubipr.htm

[104] Leo XIII, *Inscrutabili Deo Consilio* (1878). https://papalencyclicals.net/leo13/l13evl.htm

The unrestrained striving after independence…has not even spared the home, …nay, more deplorable still, it has not stopped at the steps of the sanctuary."[105]

❖ Pope Pius XI in 1922: "We have already seen and come to the conclusion that the principal cause of the confusion, restlessness, and dangers which are so prominent a characteristic of false peace is the weakening of the binding force of law and lack of respect for authority, effects which logically follow upon denial of the truth that authority comes from God, the Creator and Universal Law-giver."[106]

❖ Pope Pius XII in 1950: "Since these innumerable evils spring, as We have said, from one source only, the repudiation of God and contempt for His law, it is necessary, Venerable Brethren, to offer to God fervent prayers and recall all to those principles whence alone can

---

[105] Benedict XV, *Ad Beatissimi Apostolorum* (1914). https://papalencyclicals.net/ben15/b15adbea.htm

[106] Pius XI, *Ubi Arcano Dei Consilio* (1922). https://papalencyclicals.net/pius11/p11arcan.htm

come enlightenment for minds, peace and concord for souls and well ordered justice between the various social classes."[107]

It is not Modernism, or secret societies, or hidden plots to undermine the Church's doctrine that have introduced this crisis of faith, but something much worse. It is a collective *"non serviam"* ("I will not serve") that began in the Church and spread outward into the world, eating away at virtue and holiness for five hundred years. It is the spirit of rebellion, the spirit of self-willed independence, the same temptation that was presented to our first parents; the possibility of existing without God and deceiving ourselves into thinking we can be self-sufficient. It certainly manifested in various heretical forms and in the teachings of specific sects, but it is ultimately the result of godless ideologies influencing civilization, government, and commerce. It has reduced religion to a particular choice that individuals are free to adhere to privately, but in a world that advances on progress, materialism, and functionality, it has banished

---

[107] Pius XII, *Anni Sacri* (1950). https://papalencyclicals.net/pius12/p12anni.htm

things like contemplation, selflessness, and charity. It is the result of excluding God and all that is divine from the guiding currents of life.

This is also a hallmark of every sect or error that many who oppose the Council blame for the current situation. We might look again at the words of Pope St. Pius X in *Pascendi Dominici Gregis*, who said the Modernists "disdain all authority and brook no restraint; and relying upon a false conscience, they attempt to ascribe to a love of truth that which is in reality the result of pride and obstinacy. [...] And so they go their way, reprimands and condemnations notwithstanding[.]"[108] Or we can look to Pope Pius XI, who said the Communists "hold the principle of absolute equality, rejecting all hierarchy and divinely-constituted authority, including the authority of parents. What men call authority and subordination is derived from the community as its first and only font."[109] Even of the Freemasons, Pope Leo XIII wrote that "the reason why the legitimate liberty of

---

[108] Pius X, *Pascendi Dominici Gregis* (1907). https://papalencyclicals.net/pius10/p10pasce.htm

[109] Pius XI, *Divini Redemptoris* (1937). https://papalencyclicals.net/pius11/p11divin.htm

the Church is treated with contempt and beset with legal oppression" is because Freemasonry professes "that the Church does not possess the nature and essence of a true society, that the State has priority over it, and that civil authority takes precedence over sacred authority."[110]

The title of this book and its opening citation are taken from Pope St. Pius X's encyclical *Acerbo Nimis*. It does indeed refer to God and the supernatural, but also to the principle of authority itself, since authority is of divine origin. "Let every person be subject to the governing authorities. For there is no authority except from God, and those that exist have been instituted by God. Therefore he who resists the authorities resists what God has appointed, and those who resist will incur judgment." (Romans 13:1-2) Even Christ Himself said, "I can do nothing on my own authority...I seek not my own will but the will of him who sent me" (John 5:30). Authority in its various forms (ecclesiastical, familial, civil) flows from the authority of our Creator, and is necessarily absolute

---

[110] Leo XIII, *Inimica Vis* (1892). https://papalencyclicals.net/leo13/l13ms4.htm

and binding. As Pope Pius XI wrote in *Mit Brennender Sorge:*

> This God, this Sovereign Master, has issued commandments whose value is independent of time and space…From the fullness of the Creators' right there naturally arises the fullness of His right to be obeyed by individuals and communities, whoever they are. This obedience permeates all branches of activity in which moral values claim harmony with the law of God, and pervades all integration of the ever-changing laws of man into the immutable laws of God.[111]

Simply put, the ultimate cause of the crisis in the Church today is rejection of the very principle of authority, which starts a cascading spiral of private judgment and religious indifferentism, leading to a descent into naturalism, materialism, and eventually, a complete rejection of God. Vatican I made this very

---

[111] Pius XI, *Mit Brennender Sorge* (1937). https://papalencyclicals.net/pius11/p11brenn.htm

clear in its summary of the centuries that had preceded it, and the decades that followed bore witness to this in widespread and public fashion. As Pope Leo XIII wrote, those who "attributed to man that by the light of nature each one could know and judge concerning doctrine divinely revealed by virtue of his own reason and judgment, and that there was no necessity to submit to the authority of the Church and the Roman Pontiff" opened the door "most miserably, for denying and discarding all things and the powers of man: then insolently denying that there was any authority which emanated from God or even that there was a God[.]"[112] The popes of the last several centuries foretold what would occur if this crisis was not curbed, and their prophecies came true in the form of worldwide atheism by the 20th century.

~ ~ ~

It is at this juncture that we must pivot to respond to the charge that Vatican II is the root cause of this crisis. Critics of Vatican II may concede that these papal writings have correctly identified the root of

---

[112] Leo XIII, *Officio Sanctissimo* (1887). https://papalencyclicals.net/leo13/l13bav.htm

the crisis and will likely agree that it had been developing for quite some time before the Council. Despite this, they claim its influence had infiltrated the Church to such an extensive degree that it was the driving force behind Vatican II, and that its central errors were "actualized" at the Council. They claim the Council's declarations were either written in a deliberately ambiguous fashion to introduce heterodoxy into the Church under the guise of conciliar teaching, or that Vatican II flatly contradicts previous Church teaching.

Let us first take a moment to discuss the crisis as it appears today. What are the usual indicators of the crisis that are often spoken of in reference to Vatican II? We see low attendance at Mass, diminished belief in the Real Presence, poor or heterodox catechesis, and support for ideas the Church has soundly condemned, such as contraception, female priests, and so forth. Are these also not indicators of a rejection of Church authority and ignorance of law? Do these not indicate that the faithful rejected the teachings of the Council, as they did at Trent, and the central error lies in disobedience, not in the Church's teachings themselves?

For example, Pope Paul VI upheld the Church's perennial tradition by declaring the Church's opposition to contraception in *Humanae Vitae*, despite immense societal pressure and even pressure from those within the Church who supported the idea of revoking this teaching. (It is worth noting that the backlash to *Humanae Vitae* was so vehement and so widespread that Paul VI did not write another encyclical for the remaining 10 years he was pope.) To repurpose a quote from Pope Pius XI, "If the manner of acting of some Catholics…has left much to be desired, this has often come about because they have not known and pondered sufficiently the teachings of the Sovereign Pontiffs on these questions."[113]

The swaths of lay faithful and even religious leaving the Church after the Council may be an indicator of one of two things: that they left the Church out of dissatisfaction that the Council did not make the changes they wanted (perhaps reflecting the long-standing consumerist mindset that had been prevalent for many years), or that their faith was not anchored strongly enough to keep them within the

---

[113] Pius XI, *Divini Redemptoris* (1937). https://papalencyclicals.net/pius11/p11divin.htm

church when it was challenged (perhaps reflecting a faith that was dependent on external ritual rather than on internal truth). Whether they left the Church because of dissatisfaction or scandal, it further demonstrates that the reforms themselves were not the issue, but simply the catalyst for revealing what was already under the surface.

All the issues we have examined thus far had built up and simply needed an outlet to finally burst out into the open. The "spirit of Vatican II" ("change" in any way) finally gave this resistance and independence an excuse to come out in full force, using the Council as an excuse to push its rebellious spirit. Let us remember that the clerics who introduced the doctrinal and liturgical aberrancies in the years following the Council were formed in seminaries that adhered to "pre-conciliar" methods (not to mention that the faithful who went along with these changes were catechized with this material). Something was clearly amiss in the years before the Council.

There is one topic in particular that specifically connects to the subject of this book, one that merits a response that may perhaps at least provide material for further consideration. The objective of this book

Chapter 7: The True Source of the Crisis

is not to issue rebuttals to the various criticisms of Vatican II, and I will not attempt to do so here. But in light of our exploration of the cause of the crisis, critics will surely object that if one of the earliest indicators of the crisis is widespread religious indifferentism, this is surely proof that the crisis reached the highest levels of the Church, as per the Church's declaration on religious freedom in the document *Dignitatis Humanae*. Many believe this declaration contradicts previous teachings on religious indifferentism cited in earlier chapters. Objections on other topics such as the liturgical reform or ecumenism might say that these were legitimate aspirations that were poorly executed, but the objection to *Dignitatis Humanae* exceeds mere prudential decisions; it relates directly to Catholic doctrine.

If we believe in the dogma of indefectibility and trust in the Lord's words that the gates of Hell will not prevail against the Church, it does not seem necessary to respond to accusations that the Church could teach positive error and actively lead souls astray. If conciliar declarations seem ambiguous or unclear, it is up to the Church to clarify them (which has already occurred), and if they appear to contradict previous teachings, we ought to submit to the Church's judgment that she has issued, and trust that she knows and understands these issues better than the laity. The fact that Vatican II did not pronounce any new definitive doctrine or issue any anathemas should not affect our required submission of intellect and will to the teaching authority of the Church. As Pope Leo XIII wrote:

> In defining the limits of the obedience owed to the pastors of souls, but most of all to the authority of the Roman Pontiff, it must not be supposed that it is only to be yielded in relation to dogmas of which the obstinate denial cannot be disjoined from the crime of heresy. Nay, further, it is not enough sincerely and firmly to assent to doctrines which, though not defined by any solemn pronouncement of the Church, are by her proposed to belief, as divinely revealed, in her common and universal teaching, and which the Vatican Council declared are to be believed "with Catholic and divine faith." But

Chapter 7: The True Source of the Crisis

this likewise must be reckoned amongst the duties of Christians, that they allow themselves to be ruled and directed by the authority and leadership of bishops, and, above all, of the apostolic see. [...] *Wherefore it belongs to the Pope to judge authoritatively what things the sacred oracles contain, as well as what doctrines are in harmony, and what in disagreement, with them; and also, for the same reason, to show forth what things are to be accepted as right, and what to be rejected as worthless; what it is necessary to do and what to avoid doing, in order to attain eternal salvation.* For, otherwise, there would be no sure interpreter of the commands of God, nor would there be any safe guide showing man the way he should live.[114]

It is important to understand *Dignitatis Humanae* in the context of the Council overall. In order to effectively carry out the evangelizing mission of

---

[114] Leo XIII, *Sapientiae Christianae* (1890). https://papalencyclicals.net/leo13/l13sapie.htm

Vatican II, Catholics had to be free from external coercion or force, something they had been contending with in the form of persecutions endured over the recent decades. *Dignitatis Humanae* was not issued as a form of succumbing to modernity; it was issued so that, in order for the faithful to carry out the Church's mission, they could do so unhindered and without fear of coercion. As the document states, "Religious freedom, in turn, which men demand as necessary to fulfill their duty to worship God, has to do with immunity from coercion in civil society. Therefore it leaves untouched traditional Catholic doctrine on the moral duty of men and societies toward the true religion and toward the one Church of Christ."[115]

Religious *indifferentism* is not the same thing as religious *freedom*. The Church has never understood "freedom" to mean unrestricted license to do whatever we want. This is, in fact, the *opposite* of freedom!

---

[115] Paul VI, Declaration on Religious Freedom *Dignitatis Humanae* (1965). Vatican Archive, https://vatican.va/archive/hist_councils/ii_vatican_council/documents/vat-ii_decl_19651207_dignitatis-humanae_en.html

As Pope St. John Paul II wrote, freedom "consists not in doing what we like, but in having the right to do what we ought."[116] Repurposing this quote, religious freedom consists not in choosing what religion we like, but having the right to practice the religion that we ought.

It is worth noting that the footnotes of *Dignitatis Humanae* indicate it is clearly based on the teachings of previous encyclicals that further support this, several of which we will briefly examine. The first of these is Leo XIII's *Libertas Praestantissimum*, written in 1900, in which he states:

> And, first, let us examine that liberty in individuals which is so opposed to the virtue of religion, namely, the liberty of worship, as it is called. This is based on the principle that every man is free to profess as he may choose any religion or none. [...] Another liberty is

---

[116] Homily of His Holiness John Paul II, Sunday 8 October 1995. Vatican Archive, https://www.vatican.va/content/john-paul-ii/en/homilies/1995/documents/hf_jp-ii_hom_19951008_baltimore.html

widely advocated, namely, liberty of conscience. If by this is meant that everyone may, as he chooses, worship God or not, it is sufficiently refuted by the arguments already adduced. *But it may also be taken to mean that every man in the State may follow the will of God and, from a consciousness of duty and free from every obstacle, obey His commands. This, indeed, is true liberty, a liberty worthy of the sons of God, which nobly maintains the dignity of man and is stronger than all violence or wrong — a liberty which the Church has always desired and held most dear.*[117]

Another is Pope Pius XI's *Mit Brennender Sorge*, in which he wrote to the faithful enduring persecution in Nazi Germany: "[W]hen your faith, like gold, is being tested in the fire of tribulation and persecution, *when your religious freedom is beset on all sides*…you have every right to words of truth[.]" He further stated, "The believer has an absolute right to profess his Faith and live according to its dictates.

---

[117] Leo XIII, *Libertas Praestantissimum* (1888). https://papalencyclicals.net/leo13/l13liber.htm

Chapter 7: The True Source of the Crisis

Laws which impede this profession and practice of Faith are against natural law."[118]

The final example may be found in Pope Paul VI's *Ecclesiam Suam*, issued just one year before *Dignitatis Humanae*. Paul VI wrote the following:[119]

> Obviously we cannot share in these various forms of religion [Judaism, Islam, etc] nor can we remain indifferent to the fact that each of them, in its own way, should regard itself as being the equal of any other… *Indeed, honesty compels us to declare openly our conviction that there is but one true religion, the religion of Christianity.* It is our hope that all who seek God and adore Him may come to acknowledge its truth. But we do, nevertheless, recognize and respect the moral and spiritual values of the various non-Christian religions, *and we desire to join with them in promoting and defending common ideals of*

---

[118] Pius XI, *Mit Brennender Sorge*.

[119] Paul VI, *Ecclesiam Suam* (1964). https://papalencyclicals.net/paul06/p6eccles.htm

religious liberty, human brotherhood, good culture, social welfare and civil order.

These three examples clearly demonstrate that the Church understands religious freedom in different contexts and with different meanings, and there is an understanding of it that aligns with traditional Catholic teaching. Pope Paul VI's passage from *Ecclesiam Suam* is especially relevant, as his support for religious liberty is stated directly after he reaffirms the teachings of previous pontiffs on the error of religious indifferentism. It is rather perplexing to think he could solemnly promulgate a conciliar document which affirms an error that he himself had condemned.

As an example of religious freedom in the sense that the Council intended for it to be understood, we can look to Pope Pius XII, who applied it back onto the Church herself in *Mystici Corporis*:

> [T]hey are most certainly not genuine Christians who against their belief are forced to go into a church, to approach the altar and

to receive the Sacraments; for the "faith without which it is impossible to please God" is an entirely free "submission of intellect and will." Therefore whenever it happens, despite the constant teaching of this Apostolic See, that anyone is compelled to embrace the Catholic faith against his will, Our sense of duty demands that We condemn the act. For men must be effectively drawn to the truth by the Father of light through the Spirit of His beloved Son[.][120]

There is much that can be said about *Dignitatis Humanae*. It has been (and continues to be) debated for many years after the Council closed, and while I believe connecting it to historical precedent is important, there is another perspective from which this issue should be considered; a perspective that hopefully the previous chapters have conveyed, and which I will attempt to summarize here.

Not only is it insupportable to think that the Catholic Church could declare in an official act of a

---

[120] Pius XII, *Mystici Corporis* (1943). https://papalencyclicals.net/pius12/p12mysti.htm

general council that the Catholic religion is not the only true religion, or that all religions are equally efficacious means to salvation; it is equally insupportable to think the Church could approve of this idea when papal warnings (perhaps we might call them prophecies?) and the trajectory of history have clearly demonstrated that religious indifferentism is the first step on the path to naturalism, atheism, and abandonment of God. It is assuredly impossible to think that the Church could approve of the central error behind the crisis of faith that has afflicted the Church for centuries, or that the Holy Spirit who guides and protects the Church could allow her to succumb to such evil. As Pius XI wrote in *Mit Brennender Sorge*, "[T]he Founder of the Church, who breathed her into existence at Pentecost, cannot disown the foundations as He laid them."[121] It is simply untenable to think the Church of Jesus Christ could implicitly approve of godlessness.

It is not that Vatican II *caused* the crisis, but that it *revealed* a crisis which had been simmering for centuries, and was then exacerbated by priests and laity

---

[121] Pius XI, *Mit Brennender Sorge* (1937). https://papalencyclicals.net/pius11/p11brenn.htm

who finally had an outlet to unleash this crisis into the Church. Widespread falling away from the faith, lack of interest in spiritual things, prioritizing material gain— all of this was already present, and the popes had been warning the world for many years about it. Priests came from social circles that had been influenced by these things; should we be surprised that they openly rebelled against the Church and its teachings after the Council? (As has been shown, the popes had not only warned about the spirit of the age impacting the laity, but the priesthood as well. In 1906, Pope St. Pius X wrote to the bishops of Italy about a "cause...of very serious importance" which "demands all the attention of [their] mind and all the energy of [their] pastoral office to counteract[.]" This was the "spirit of insubordination and independence displayed...among the clergy" and an "an open contempt for authority and for those who exercise it," a spirit which was "doing the damage especially among young priests, spreading among them new and reprehensible theories concerning the very nature of obedience."[122])

---

[122] Pius X, *Pieni L'Animo* (1906). https://papalencyclicals.net/pius10/p10clr.htm

If we take these papal warnings seriously, we may also consider the potential state of the Church and the world if Vatican II had never occurred. How long would the internal decay of the crisis have had to grow under a pious surface before individuals determined this crisis necessitated a response in the form of an independent ministry, as some do today? How many priests and bishops would have had to succumb to the world and its attractions before other priests determined they needed to intervene? In what more dire ways might this crisis have manifested? If Vatican II is the cause, as some claim, then the crisis should be resolved when the Council is nullified, but it certainly would not disappear upon the erasure of a series of documents, thereby demonstrating that the issue runs deeper. The fact that these evils came to light *after* the Council does not mean they came *because of* the Council. And just as they had developed over many years beforehand, they will take many years afterward to curb. But this can and will be done.

Chapter 8

Toward a Solution

Wilt thou not revive us again, that thy people may rejoice in thee? (Ps 85:6)

Thus far, we have expounded at length on the causes of the crisis, and we know that the Magisterium has directly identified the root cause. But it does no good to lament the tidal wave of errors that we face if there is no solution that can be presented. As Pope Gregory XVI wrote in *Mirari Vos*, "It is not enough for Us to deplore these innumerable evils unless We strive to uproot them."[123] And just as the Magisterium has exposed the crisis at its core, it has also indicated what can be done to remedy it.

As should be very clear, the solution is not to redact the Council. Assuming this were even possible after it was solemnly promulgated by the supreme

---

[123] Gregory XVI, *Mirari Vos* (1832). https://papalencyclicals.net/greg16/g16mirar.htm

authority, accepted by the bishops of the world, confirmed by every subsequent pope, and has served as the basis of the Church's activity for the last 60 years, we cannot expect that turning back is a better solution than forging ahead, especially not at the behest of the laity instead of by the authority of the Holy See.

Let us again briefly turn to John XXIII, who wrote in *Humanae Salutis*:[124]

> Our first announcement of the Council…was like a little seed that we planted with anxious mind and hand. Supported by heavenly help, we set about the complex and delicate work of preparation. In the three years since we have day by day seen the little seed develop and become, by God's blessing, a great tree. As we look back on the long and tiring journey, a hymn of thanksgiving to God rises from our heart that he has been so

---

[124] "Pope John XXIII Convokes the Second Vatican Council," trans. Joseph A. Komonchak, https://jakomonchak.wordpress.com/wp-content/uploads/2011/12/humanae-salutis.pdf

generous in his help that everything has unfolded in a suitable way and in harmony of spirit.

This "tree" of the Council was planted "to offer a possibility for all men of good will to turn their thoughts and proposals toward peace, a peace which can and must come above all from spiritual and supernatural realities, from human intelligence and conscience enlightened and guided by God, Creator and Redeemer of humanity."[125]

How well do Pius XI's words from *Mit Brennender Sorge* apply here!

> If, then, the tree of peace, which we planted…with the purest intention, has not brought forth the fruit, which…We had fondly hoped, no one in the world who has eyes to see and ears to hear will be able to lay the blame on the Church and on her Head. [...] In the furrows, where We tried to sow the seed of a sincere peace, other men — the "enemy" of Holy Scripture — oversowed the

---

[125] Ibid.

cockle of distrust, unrest, hatred, defamation, of a determined hostility overt or veiled, fed from many sources and wielding many tools, against Christ and His Church. [...] The Church, whose work lies among men and operates through men, may see her divine mission obscured by human, too human, combination, persistently growing and developing like the cockle among the wheat of the Kingdom of God.[126]

The passage about the wheat and the weeds is worth revisiting in its full context:

Another parable he put before them, saying, "The kingdom of heaven may be compared to a man who sowed good seed in his field; but while men were sleeping, his enemy came and sowed weeds among the wheat, and went away. So when the plants came up and bore grain, then the weeds appeared also. And the servants of the householder came

---

[126] Pius XI, *Mit Brennender Sorge* (1937). https://papalencyclicals.net/pius11/p11brenn.htm

Chapter 8: Toward a Solution

>and said to him, 'Sir, did you not sow good seed in your field? How then has it weeds?' He said to them, 'An enemy has done this.' *The servants said to him, 'Then do you want us to go and gather them?' But he said, 'No; lest in gathering the weeds you root up the wheat along with them. Let both grow together until the harvest; and at harvest time I will tell the reapers, Gather the weeds first and bind them in bundles to be burned, but gather the wheat into my barn.'"* (Matthew 13:24-30)

As stated, there are those who believe we must simply till up the entire field, wheat and weeds together, and admit that the attempt at sowing was a mistake. But surely all can agree that even if the Council were nullified, the world would still be plagued by all the previously described issues, and the Church would attempt to face them as she had before, which did not hold them back and certainly would not now, when these issues have only worsened in the last 60 years. The crisis sprouted, grew, and entangled the Church and the world, undaunted by condemnations and anathemas, and breaking down with brute force the walls of spiritual defenses. Many of the previously cited encyclicals recommend drastic actions to deter the growth of the crisis, but it persisted despite all these things. Even if there is disagreement on the source and the resolution of the crisis, all can certainly agree that it had been developing for a long time before Vatican II, and "traditional Catholicism" did not hold it at bay. Continuing with the methods and the approaches the Church had been following over the last several hundred years is not the answer.

We must let both the wheat and weeds grow until the harvest time. Even if the weeds seem to choke out the wheat, there is indeed wheat there. This growth of new life in the Church is not something that will happen immediately, but it will happen nonetheless. Vatican II is part of the Church's past now, and whatever agendas were attempted to be forced in, whatever misrepresentations were presented, whatever was done in the name of the Council that the Church did not intend, it does not and cannot erase the Council from our history.

Secondly, as the previous chapter has made clear, the root of this crisis is disregard of authority. As much as we may be tempted to navigate this crisis on our own, it must be stated— trying to navigate our way through this crisis independently of the Church cannot be the solution. A council was called, and its declarations were passed almost universally. What resulted was a disaster caused by things that critics of the Council are quick to point out were not even called for by it. Some thought the Council did not go far enough, and took its intentions for "updating" Church discipline and applied it to their own desires, perhaps for things they thought the Church was going to approve and did not, or for things they thought were applicable to modern times. Others, seeing the chaos, blamed the Council directly, and felt it necessary to simply ignore it and its directives. Laxity in discipline, heterodox teachings, and confusion began with disobedience to the Council; the reaction to this was also rooted in disobedience. Should it not be obvious that neither of these things will solve the crisis?

If the Church cannot overcome this crisis on her own, as some believe, they certainly cannot expect to do it on their own. As Pius XII made clear in his *Guiding Principles for the Lay Apostolate*, "We are nevertheless aware that the present crisis is above all a spiritual crisis. Today as always, men hunger for God. *The solution which we must give is not our own, but Christ's communicated through the Church.*"[127] Would this not display the same spirit of independence and self-sufficiency that the Holy See has so frequently deplored in its examination of the crisis? If the Church has been "compromised" and is unable to effectively combat this crisis, how can individuals expect to do it without her (or against her)? We *need* the Church and her authority to make any sort of impact. As Pius XI wrote, "Because the Church is by divine institution the sole depository and interpreter of the ideals and teachings of Christ, she alone possesses in any complete and true sense the power effectively to combat that…which has already done and, still threatens, such tremendous harm to the home and to the state."[128]

What, then, *is* the solution?

---

[127] Pius XII, *Guiding Principles for the Lay Apostolate* (1957). https://papalencyclicals.net/pius12/ p12layap.htm

[128] Pius XI, *Ubi Arcano Dei Consilio* (1922). https://papalencyclicals.net/pius11/p11arcan.htm

Chapter 8: Toward a Solution

Let us begin by turning to Pope Leo XIII, who wrote the following in *Tametsi Futura Prospicientibus* (1900):

> We have but too much evidence of the value and result of a morality divorced from divine faith. How is it that, in spite of all the zeal for the welfare of the masses, nations are in such straits and even distress, and that the evil is daily on the increase? We are told that society is quite able to help itself; that it can flourish without the assistance of Christianity, and attain its end by its own unaided efforts. Public administrators prefer a purely secular system of government. All traces of the religion of our forefathers are daily disappearing from political life and administration. What blindness! Once the idea of the authority of God as the Judge of right and wrong is forgotten, law must necessarily lose its primary authority and justice must perish: and these are the two most powerful and most necessary bonds of society. Similarly,

once the hope and expectation of eternal happiness is taken away, temporal goods will be greedily sought after. Every man will strive to secure the largest share for himself. Hence arise envy, jealousy, hatred. The consequences are conspiracy, anarchy, nihilism. So great is this struggle of the passions and so serious the dangers involved, that we must either anticipate ultimate ruin or seek for an efficient remedy.[129]

Consider that this was written at the very beginning of the 20th century, before the world had erupted into war and progressed to great lengths of scientific progress. How much more applicable are these words to our present day!

Leo XIII continues: "It is of course both right and necessary to punish malefactors, to educate the masses, and by legislation to prevent crime in every possible way: but all this is by no means sufficient.

---

[129] Leo XIII, *Tametsi Futura Prospicientibus* (1900). https://papalencyclicals.net/leo13/l13tamet.htm

The salvation of the nations must be looked for higher."[130]

This is a very important and wise insight by Pope Leo in his proposal for a solution. True reform and restoration cannot be accomplished through "negative" means such as punishment and condemnations. These are, of course, vital when necessary, but trying to uproot disbelief and pride through issuing anathemas and corrections in a world that holds very little regard for any form of authority is quite counterproductive. We can look to the First Vatican Council as an example, which issued a total of 22 anathemas (many of them related to erroneous ideas about divine revelation and human reason), but which did not slow the spread of the crisis in the decades that followed.

And this is precisely why Vatican II did not issue any anathemas. As Pope John XXIII said in his opening address to Vatican II, "Today, however, Christ's Bride…believes that, present needs are best served by explaining more fully the purport of her doctrines,

---

[130] Ibid.

rather than by publishing condemnations."[131] The objectives of the Council could hardly be accomplished by relying on denunciations in a time when even many within the Church disregarded her authority, let alone those who were not part of the Church. Restoration of morality and discipline would have to be fostered through teaching, leading, and example, not forced through reprimands.

Pope Leo XIII continued as follows in *Tametsi Futura Prospicientibus*:

> A power greater than human must be called in to teach men's hearts, awaken in them the sense of duty, and make them better. This is the power which once before saved the world from destruction when groaning under much more terrible evils. Once remove all impediments and allow the Christian spirit to revive and grow strong in a nation, and that nation will be healed. The strife between the classes and the masses will die

---

[131] Pope Saint John XXIII, "Opening Address To the Council", Catholic Culture, https://www.catholicculture.org/culture/library/view.cfm?recnum=3233

away; mutual rights will be respected. If Christ be listened to, both rich and poor will do their duty. The former will realise that they must observe justice and charity, the latter self-restraint and moderation, if both are to be saved. Domestic life will be firmly established by the salutary fear of God as the Lawgiver. In the same way the precepts of the natural law, which dictates respect for lawful authority and obedience to the laws, will exercise their influence over the people. Seditions and conspiracies will cease. Wherever Christianity rules over all without let or hindrance there the order established by Divine Providence is preserved, and both security and prosperity are the happy result.

The common welfare, then, urgently demands a return to Him from whom we should never have gone astray; to Him who is the Way, the Truth, and the Life,-and this on the part not only of individuals but of society as a whole. We must restore Christ to this His own rightful possession. All elements of the national life must be made to drink in the Life which proceedeth from Him—legislation, political institutions, education, marriage and family life, capital and labour. Everyone must see that the very growth of civilisation which is so ardently desired depends greatly upon this, since it is fed and grows not so much by material wealth and prosperity, as by the spiritual qualities of morality and virtue.[132]

As Pope Leo declared, and as his successors would confirm, the solution to this crisis of faith is to restore morality to public life by rejuvenating the Christian spirit in civilization. The answer lies in an undaunted embodiment of virtues such as obedience, humility, poverty, and charity, and a bold witness to the faith in our words and actions to show the world that Christ is the fulfillment of all its desires. As Pope Pius XI confirmed in *Divini Redemptoris*, "As in all the stormy periods of the history of the Church, the fundamental remedy today lies in a sincere renewal of private and public life according to

---

[132] Leo XIII, *Tametsi Futura Prospicientibus* (1900). https://papalencyclicals.net/leo13/l13tamet.htm

the principles of the Gospel by all those who belong to the Fold of Christ, that they may be in truth the salt of the earth to preserve human society from total corruption."[133]

And this is *exactly* why Vatican II was called— to rejuvenate the Church's missionary activity and to bring the light of the Gospel to a world lost in spiritual darkness. Pope John XXIII had written in his 1959 encyclical *Ad Petri Cathedram* that the Council was summoned so that "the hearts of men would be stirred to a fuller and deeper recognition of truth, a renewal of Christian morals, and a restoration of unity, harmony, and peace[.]"[134] By choosing not to focus on the finer points of doctrine, and rather encouraging a return to fundamental Gospel principles, the Church reminded its members of Christ's mandate to go forth and preach to all nations, and issued a universal call to holiness to meet the modern age.

---

[133] Pius XI, *Divini Redemptoris* (1937). https://papalencyclicals.net/pius11/p11divin.htm

[134] John XXIII, *Ad Petri Cathedram* (1959). https://papalencyclicals.net/john23/j23petri.htm

Chapter 9

Salt and Light

All the ends of the earth shall remember and turn to the Lord; and all the families of the nations shall worship before him. (Ps 22:27)

Our time is one of great opportunities for the Church. Never has the world had such abundant possibilities to grow closer to God through the wide array of resources that modern technology lays at our feet. Never has there been such a need for a restoration of Christian values, when the world has sunken to the mire of self-gratification for so long. Never was there a greater need for the entire Church to mobilize together and offer the love and peace of Christ to the furthest reaches of creation. To use the words of Pope Pius XII, "If things have gone wrong on account of the desertion from Christ, public and private life must return to Him as soon as possible: if error has clouded the minds of men, they must return to that truth which, revealed from on high, indicates the right way to heaven: if hatred has brought them fatal results, they must return to Christian love which alone can heal their many wounds, and carry them over the crisis so filled with danger."[135]

How can we most effectively put into action what the Magisterium has recommended as the solution?

To continue our examination of Leo XIII's *Tametsi Futura Prospicientibus*:

> *It is rather ignorance than ill-will which keeps multitudes away from Jesus Christ.* There are many who study humanity and the natural world; few who study the Son of God. The first step, then, is to substitute knowledge for ignorance, so that He may no longer be despised or rejected because He is unknown. We conjure all Christians throughout the world to strive all they can to know their Redeemer as He really is. The more one contemplates Him with sincere and unprejudiced mind, the clearer does it become that there can be nothing more salutary than His law, more divine than His teaching. [...] You must

---

[135] Pius XII, *Optatissima Pax* (1947). https://papalencyclicals.net/pius12/p12optat.htm

> look upon it as a chief part of your duty to engrave upon the minds of your people the true knowledge, the very likeness of Jesus Christ; to illustrate His charity, His mercies, His teaching, by your writings and your words, in schools, in Universities, from the pulpit; wherever opportunity is offered you. The world has heard enough of the so-called "rights of man." Let it hear something of the rights of God.[136]

The solution does not reside in a particular liturgical form, practices of piety, or specific theological outlooks. The solution is not a *thing*; it is a *person*, Christ Himself, who we as members of the Mystical Body bring to the world when we are united in the bonds of peace and charity, not only preaching His words but living them out. This is our commission given to us by the Church— to show through our words and especially our actions that Christ can offer

---

[136] Leo XIII, *Tametsi Futura Prospicientibus* (1900). https://papalencyclicals.net/leo13/l13tamet.htm

what all truly seek. What, then, must we do to effectively bring Christ to the world, as the Church has commissioned us to do?

First and foremost, we must recognize that obedience and submission to authority are paramount. If this crisis came about because of disobedience, it is only through obedience that it can be resolved. In the vast range of encyclicals cited herein, the Holy See has issued constant reminders that obedience and unity are critical to combat the rebellious spirit that was driving this crisis. From Pius VI ("Persuade them that subjects ought to keep faith and show obedience to those who by God's ordering lead and rule them"[137]), to Leo XII ("Teach your people great reverence for the Church's authority which has been directly established by God"[138]), to Pius IX ("[F]oster in all men…their obedience towards this See of Peter…See to it with similar firmness that the most holy laws of the Church are observed"[139]) and beyond, the

---

[137] Pius VI, *Inscrutabile* (1775). https://papalencyclicals.net/pius06/p6inscru.htm

[138] Leo XII, *Ubi Primum* (1824). https://papalencyclicals.net/leo12/l12ubipr.htm

[139] Pius IX, *Qui Pluribus* (1846). https://papalencyclicals.net/pius09/p9quiplu.htm

Church has constantly reminded the faithful that our duty is to obey our lawful superiors to maintain the concord and peace that is so necessary for the Church to flourish.

A fuller explanation of how obedience relates to the present situation may be found in Pope Benedict XV's encyclical *Ad Beatissimi Apostolorum:*

> The success of every society of men, for whatever purpose it is formed, is bound up with the harmony of the members in the interests of the common cause. Hence We must devote Our earnest endeavours to appease dissension and strife, of whatever character, amongst Catholics, and to prevent new dissensions arising, so that there may be unity of ideas and of action amongst all. The enemies of God and of the Church are perfectly well aware that any internal quarrel amongst Catholics is a real victory for them. Hence it is their usual practice when they see Catholics strongly united, to endeavour by cleverly sowing the seeds of discord, to break up that

union. And would that the result had not frequently justified their hopes, to the great detriment of the interests of religion! Hence, therefore, whenever legitimate authority has once given a clear command, let no one transgress that command, because it does not happen to commend itself to him; but let each one subject his own opinion to the authority of him who is his superior, and obey him as a matter of conscience. Again, let no private individual, whether in books or in the press, or in public speeches, take upon himself the position of an authoritative teacher in the Church.

Let all the members of societies which further the interests of God and His Church ever remember the words of Divine Wisdom: "An obedient man shall speak of victory" (Prov. xxi. 8), for unless they obey God by showing deference to the Head of the Church, vainly will they look for divine assistance, vainly, too, will they labour.

The spirit of insubordination and independence, so characteristic of our times, has, as We deplored above, not entirely spared the ministers of the Sanctuary. It is not rare for pastors of the Church to find sorrow and contradiction where they had a right to look for comfort and help. Let those who have so unfortunately failed in their duty, recall to their minds again and again, that the authority of those whom "the Holy Spirit hath placed as Bishops to rule the Church of God" (Acts xx. 28) is a divine authority. Let them remember that if, as we have seen, those who resist any legitimate authority, resist God, much more impiously do they act who refuse to obey the Bishop, whom God has consecrated with a special character by the exercise of His power.[140]

Just as the seed of disobedience ultimately sprouted into an imposing growth of atheism, the seed of obedience will restore the right alignment of morality, growing first in individuals, then families,

---

[140] Benedict XV, *Ad Beatissimi Apostolorum* (1914). https://papalencyclicals.net/ben15/b15adbea.htm

then communities and government and finally nations, guided by the Church. Obedience necessitates union of mind and heart with the Church, to unite our purposes with hers so that the effort to combat the crisis will be characterized by unity. No true restoration can be rooted in the spirit of independence and resistance.

Next, recalling Vatican II's intention to avoid disputing theological subtleties or fine-tuning doctrine, we must remember that public and private morality is influenced by action and by example. Doctrinal discourse certainly has its place, but in a world which sees no functional value in religion, our undaunted witness to a faith that appears radically countercultural will do much more to influence the average person than debates will. A genuine display of virtue guiding our actions will prompt curiosity into what brings such joy in a world beset by anxieties and worry. We may once again look to Pope St. Pius X, who recommended this course of action at the very beginning of the 20th century. His 1903 encyclical *E Supremi* says the following:

Chapter 9: Salt and Light

[W]e must use every means and exert all our energy to bring about the utter disappearance of the enormous and detestable wickedness, so characteristic of our time — the substitution of man for God; this done, it remains to restore to their ancient place of honor the most holy laws and counsels of the gospel; to proclaim aloud the truths taught by the Church, and her teachings on the sanctity of marriage, on the education and discipline of youth, on the possession and use of property, the duties that men owe to those who rule the State; and lastly to restore equilibrium between the different classes of society according to Christian precept and custom.

But in order that...Christ may be formed in all, be it remembered, Venerable Brethren, that no means is more efficacious than charity. *"For the Lord is not in the earthquake" (III Kings xix., II) — it is vain to hope to attract souls to God by a bitter zeal.* [...] Who will prevent us from hoping that the flame of Christian charity may dispel the darkness from their minds and bring to them light and the peace of God?

For truly it is of little avail to discuss questions with nice subtlety, or to discourse eloquently of rights and duties, when all this is unconnected with practice. *The times we live in demand action — but action which consists entirely in observing with fidelity and zeal the divine laws and the precepts of the Church, in the frank and open profession of religion, in the exercise of every kind of charitable works, without regard to self interest or worldly advantage.* Such luminous examples given by the great army of soldiers of Christ will be of much greater avail in moving and drawing men than words and sublime dissertations; and it will easily come about that when human respect has been driven out, and prejudices and doubting laid aside, large numbers will be won to Christ, becoming in their turn promoters of His knowledge and love which are the road to true and solid happiness.[141]

A public rejection of faith demands a public demonstration of faith to counteract it. We should not devote our time and energy to debating the finer points of doctrine when we could be acting as a witness to those who have no knowledge of the faith at all. As Pope St. Pius X further wrote in his 1905 encyclical *Acerbo Nimis*, catechetical instruction is not done through obscure and lengthy teachings, but through good example.

> The task of the catechist is to take up one or other of the truths of faith or of Christian morality and then explain it in all its parts; and since amendment of life is the chief aim of his instruction, the catechist must needs make a comparison between what God commands us to do and what is our actual con-

---

[141] Pius X, *E Supremi* (1903). https://papalencyclicals.net/pius10/p10supre.htm

duct. After this, he will use examples appropriately taken from the Holy Scriptures, Church history, and the lives of the saints — thus moving his hearers and clearly pointing out to them how they are to regulate their own conduct.[142]

A final necessity in our apostolic work of today is to uphold a spirit of poverty and charity. As we have seen, the Magisterium has identified violence, enmity, and war as the fruits of this materialistic spirit that has grown over the centuries. In his condemnation of Communism and the greed at its core, Pope Pius XI wrote that poverty and charity are the most effective remedies for rampant materialism and the animosity that derives from it.

> We wish, Venerable Brethren, to insist…on two teachings of Our Lord which have a special bearing on the present condition of the human race: detachment from earthly goods and the precept of charity. […]

---

[142] Pius X, *Acerbo Nimis* (1905). https://papalencyclicals.net/pius10/p10chdoc.htm

All Christians, rich or poor, must keep their eye fixed on heaven, remembering that "we have not here a lasting city, but we seek one that is to come." The rich should not place their happiness in things of earth nor spend their best efforts in the acquisition of them.

But the poor too, in their turn, while engaged, according to the laws of charity and justice, in acquiring the necessities of life and also in bettering their condition, should always remain "poor in spirit," and hold spiritual goods in higher esteem than earthly property and pleasures. Let them remember that the world will never be able to rid itself of misery, sorrow and tribulation, which are the portion even of those who seem most prosperous. Patience, therefore, is the need of all, that Christian patience which comforts the heart with the divine assurance of eternal happiness.

Still more important as a remedy for the evil we are considering, or certainly more directly calculated to cure it, is the precept of charity.

To be sure of eternal life...it is imperative to return to a more moderate way of life, to renounce the joys, often sinful, which the world today holds out in such abundance; to forget self for love of the neighbor. There is a divine regenerating force in this "new precept" (as Christ called it) of Christian charity. Its faithful observance will pour into the heart an inner peace which the world knows not, and will finally cure the ills which oppress humanity.[143]

The Magisterium, in its wisdom, has spoken words of clarity for many years about the current crisis of faith. If a lack of Christian principles in public life is one of the causes, the embodiment of virtue is the answer. If the love of money and amassing of wealth is the cause, the solution is a return to Gospel

---

[143] Pius XI, *Divini Redemptoris* (1937). https://papalencyclicals.net/pius11/p11divin.htm

Chapter 9: Salt and Light

principles of poverty, charity, and selflessness. If rejection of authority is the cause, it naturally follows that the solution is to recognize that the Church does have real authority which we are bound to obey.

We will conclude our presentation of the Magisterium's analysis with a final quotation from Pope Pius XII:

> Once the bitterness and the cruel strifes of the present have ceased, the new order of the world, of national and international life, must rest no longer on the quicksands of changeable and ephemeral standards that depend only on the selfish interests of groups and individuals. No, they must rest on the unshakable foundation, on the solid rock of natural law and of Divine Revelation.
>
> If it is to have any effect, the reeducation of mankind must be, above all things, spiritual and religious. Hence, it must proceed from Christ as from its indispensable foundation; must be actuated by justice and crowned by charity.

With a heart torn by the sufferings and afflictions of so many of her sons, but with the courage and the stability that come from the promises of Our Lord, the Spouse of Christ goes to meet the gathering storms. This she knows, that the truth which she preaches, the charity which she teaches and practices, will be the indispensable counselors and aids to men of good will in the reconstruction of a new world based on justice and love[.][144]

There is real cause for hope in our present time. Despite the challenges the Church has faced, she is and has always remained the spotless Bride of Christ, guided by the Holy Spirit to navigate whatever threats the world can conjure. We may find reassurance in the words of Pope St. Pius X, who wrote, "Whether the wicked will it or not, God makes even error aid in the triumph of Truth whose guardian and defender is the Church. He puts corruption in the service of sanctity, whose mother and nurse is the

---

[144] Pius XII, *Summi Pontificatus* (1939). https://papalencyclicals.net/pius12/p12summi.htm

Church. Out of persecution He brings a more wondrous 'freedom from our enemies.' For these reasons, when worldly men think they see the Church buffeted and almost capsized in the raging storm, then she really comes forth fairer, stronger, purer, and brighter with the lustre of distinguished virtues."[145] We ought to take consolation in the fact that the Catholic Church has not cowed to the pressure of modernity in the way most (if not all) other Christian denominations have in recent times. Through the visible signs of unity, most especially the Eucharist and the papacy, the Church continues to be a beacon of truth to guide us through the fog of our time.

Overcoming this crisis may be a lofty goal. It may seem too vast or too difficult. Just as the crisis festered for hundreds of years, the solution may take hundreds of years to effectively implement. "It may be that the fruit of our labors may be slow in coming, but charity wearies not with waiting, knowing that God prepares His rewards not for the results of toil

---

[145] Pius X, *Editae Sapae* (1910). https://papalencyclicals.net/pius10/p10cha.htm

but for the good will shown in it."[146] This is our calling as Catholics today; to "go forth" and announce the Gospel to the world, to bring Christ to a world that is desperate for truth even if it does not know it. It is our responsibility to be "the salt of the earth" and "the light of the world" (Matthew 5:13, 14), however small our individual efforts may seem. It is our task to embody the virtues and be faithful witnesses to Christ, so that no crisis of faith can ever overcome our hope, our joy, and our peace.

---

[146] Pius X, *E Supremi* (1903). https://papalencyclicals.net/pius10/p10supre.htm

www.ingramcontent.com/pod-product-compliance
Lightning Source LLC
LaVergne TN
LVHW020929090426
835512LV00020B/3275